PEOPLE MANAGEMENT #101

BY

STEVE SMETHURST

Copyright © Steve Smethurst 2016
This book is sold subject to the condition that it shall not, by way of trade or otherwise, be lent, resold, hired out, or otherwise circulated without the publisher's prior consent in any form of binding or cover other than that in which it is published and without a similar condition including this condition being imposed on the subsequent publisher.
The moral right of Steve Smethurst has been asserted.
ISBN-13: 978-1540845627
ISBN-10: 1540845621

This book has not been created to be specific to any individual's or organizations' situation or needs. Every effort has been made to make this book as accurate as possible. This book should serve only as a general guide and not as the ultimate source of subject information. This book contains information that might be dated and is intended only to educate and entertain. The author shall have no liability or responsibility to any person or entity regarding any loss or damage incurred, or alleged to have incurred, directly or indirectly, by the information contained in this book.

CONTENTS

HOW TO USE THIS BOOK 1
ACCOUNTABILITY 7
HUMAN BEHAVIOUR 13
ESSENTIAL BEHAVIOURAL SKILLS 28
CONSEQUENCES 48
NOTE TAKING 58
PLANNING 66
THE TECHNIQUES 73
DELEGATION 77
REVIEWING PROGRESS 93
GIVING PRAISE OR RECOGNITION 104
INTRODUCING CHANGE 116
RESPONDING TO CONCERNS OR COMPLAINTS
.... 126
PERFORMANCE MANAGEMENT 144
ADDITIONAL APPLICATIONS 163
BEHAVIOUR MANAGEMENT 165
TAKING FOLLOW UP ACTION 180
TAKING DISCIPLINARY ACTION 192
DISMISSAL 208

HOW TO USE THIS BOOK

This may sound an obvious thing to say, but **read it**.

I know managers are always seeking to save time, but don't skimp on reading every word. You will find that every element of the book is linked into a coherent overall system of managing. Don't try to cherry-pick individual items because this may lead you to miss out on the overall structure.

The programme is a coherent, holistic set of principles, knowledge and procedures. You are going to need all of it when you go live. Writing and reading are linear processes. I can't tell you everything at once, so I will have to rely on you to piece it all together.

You will find as you read through the material that a lot of it is just plain general knowledge and common sense. Please don't dismiss it as something that you can safely gloss over, or as so obvious that it's not worth giving much thought to. **Agreeing** that something is obviously worth doing and **actually**

doing it are two separate things.

This book is effectively a distilled version of the training programme that I have developed and run over the last twenty years. Because it is a book and not a three day event, there are some things that it cannot give you. Principal among these is the direct intervention and guidance of a trainer to help you put your knowledge and skill into practice.

It is a self-teach manual, so this means you have to take on the role of the trainer yourself. Although the structured interactions are designed to be easily learned and memorable, this does not mean that you will be able to pick up the techniques and run with them without any practice. If you try this, you are likely to find that as soon as something becomes difficult you will revert to whatever techniques you were using before you obtained this book.

In the classroom I spend most of my time guiding the delegates' planning and implementation so that I can be sure that they are able to use this style of management in a practice environment before they are safe to be let loose on real people.

Also in the classroom I can take every opportunity that arises to remind delegates of how the various components of the programme fit together into one holistic system. Those opportunities do not exist when the learner is a remote reader. So, all I can do is urge you to read all the material and hope that you remember to apply all of the background information in Section 1. to the planning and execution of the management processes in Sections 2. and 3.

I would be disappointed, and so would you, if you were to attempt to manage anybody based on a single cursory reading of the appropriate process. Even a skilled practitioner needs to spend some time on planning and rehearsal before each interaction. The need for preparation is even greater when you are trying out these techniques for the first time. Teaching yourself involves a lot more than just reading the words. In fact, if you just read the words, you will find that most of what is said is just straightforward common sense. So you will tend to just glide through the text agreeing with everything you see, and then thinking that you can go straight into applying it all to a real-life management situation. If you try this, I can guarantee that you will fail. Then you will blame the material and give up.

Teaching yourself, literally, involves playing the role of tutor and student simultaneously. You will need to work through the exercises given, and also use them as models for creating your own exercises, based on your specific circumstances.

You will need to plan each management interaction according to the steps identified, even to the extent of writing a script based on your proposed input and the other person's likely response. Then you will need to rehearse until you are comfortable with the structure and content of the interaction.

Believe me, there is a major difference between having the words right in your head and being able to say them, as planned, out loud. Ideally, find a friend or colleague to act out the role of the person being managed, and give honest feedback and suggestions about your performance. If you don't have anyone who can help you, you will need to practice on your own and assess your performance yourself.

What I am about to recommend may sound a little weird, and it will certainly feel weird the first time you try it but, whatever, it does work.

Before going into any people-management interaction you need to have had the experience of saying your planned words out loud to another person, so that in the real-life situation you are doing it mostly from memory. The structure of the various interactions explained in each section gives you a guaranteed format for achieving a positive outcome, but your own words are what drive the interaction along. So planning and rehearsal are essential.

You cannot gain the level of confidence required by practicing your words in front of a mirror because the image of yourself does not behave like a real person. You are only practicing half of the interaction, and the memory of talking to a picture of yourself will get you confused when you talk to a real person.

Here is the weird bit. Get a couple of action-figures, dolls, sock-puppets, anything will do, even just your hands making mouth movements. One represents you, the other is the person being managed. Say your planned words out loud through your puppet, and say the other person's anticipated response through the other puppet.

I would recommend that you find somewhere private to do this; you don't want people thinking you are crazy.

You are likely to find that on the first couple of attempts the words simply will not come out as planned. You forget what you were going to say, when you were going to say it, or how you wanted to say it. Try it first with your script. Try it again without the script. Try it again until either you can say the words you planned, or find some equally effective alternative if the planned words don't really work. Give yourself some honest feedback about your effectiveness, and also try to hear your words from the other person's point of view, i.e. how would you feel if those words were said to you.

When your puppets can get through the whole interaction faultlessly, do it one more time for luck and then you are ready to face the real world.

All of this might sound like a lot of work for what is essentially a fairly short interaction. Well, yes it is. But, you are supposed to be a people-manager and most of your time and effort should go into things to do with managing people.

At first you will find that the Pareto 80/20 rule applies (80% preparation, 20% execution). After a while the rule will reverse (20% preparation, 80% execution), but no matter how proficient you become I would urge you not to try getting by with zero preparation.

ACCOUNTABILITY

It is a fundamental principle of this programme that **people are accountable for their behaviour**. This apparently simple statement needs to be unpicked in order to ascertain its full meaning and its implications for how you go about managing people.

Behaviour

This is what people do or say. They are accountable only for their behaviour; not their thoughts or beliefs. "Attitude" can be inferred from behaviour, but the inference cannot be guaranteed to be correct. You can only manage observed behaviour.

Their behaviour

People can only be held accountable for their own behaviour, not anybody else's.

Accountable

They can be asked to give an account of their behaviour, including a statement of their reasons.

This concept of accountability provides the justification for all the recommended managerial actions in this programme.

As a manager, you have people who are accountable to you for what they do. That is to say, there are certain activities that they are obliged to undertake by virtue of having a specific job, and you have a right to ask them any questions relating to their performance or behaviour in that job.

Some accountabilities are inherent in the job from the outset. Others are acquired by making commitments to perform specific actions.

In a business or organisational context, a person's job accountabilities are few in number, and quite simple:

1. To be at the designated workplace every day, on time, and for the agreed amount of time.
2. To perform their work in accordance with expected standards and volumes.
3. To co-operate with other staff in achieving organisational goals.

4. To communicate information needed by their manager or colleagues.
5. To support and implement the organisational policy.

As their manager you have the right to expect them to do these things all the time, and to require them to give a reason if they fail to do so.

A manager has extra accountabilities: i.e. things they can be asked about by their manager.

1. To ensure that staff are aware of their accountabilities.
2. To obtain and supply information on team performance.
3. To investigate problems and take remedial action.
4. To maintain, and improve team performance.

An effective people-manager should spend most of their time finding out whether people are fulfilling their accountabilities, not by intrusive observation, but by using the opportunities for questioning afforded by the structured interactions contained in this programme.

This concept of managing accountability contains no element of the blameworthiness that is usually implied in common usage of the term "accountability", particularly in its use by the media.

Management is not primarily about finding people to punish for mistakes or omissions. Management is about finding out whether things are being done properly, and if you find that they are not, taking remedial action.

Of course, you may uncover a situation in which someone has done something wrong out of malice or incompetence which may lead to a separate management activity, but your prime focus as a manager is simply to obtain people's accounts.

As a manager you need to foster an atmosphere in which people feel able to admit to mistakes, errors of judgement, lack of skill, or occasional stupidity without the fear of incurring a punishment.

The practical reason for this is that if people experience a negative consequence for giving you a true account, they will soon stop giving you the true story and will only tell you what they feel it is safe to disclose.

Asking for an account is the first stage of an investigative problem-solving process; it is not a punishment, although it may be an uncomfortable experience. While there may be evidence that someone has not met their accountabilities, until they have given you their account (stated their reasons) it is wiser to assume that there is a real reason which can be identified and corrected if necessary.

People will vary in the degree to which they are willing to give a full account depending on their prior experience with other managers, so with some you may have a lengthy process of getting them used to the idea that they can safely tell you everything you need to know without fear of recrimination. Once you have convinced them of this you will be amazed at the effect it has on their productivity.

They will no longer fear their interactions with management, and will approach each meeting as a collaborative reporting and problem-solving session.

Consolidation:

1. Make a list of people who are accountable to you for some or all of their behaviour. These are most likely to be your subordinates, but may also include colleagues, suppliers or customers, who you expect to do something for you.

2. For each person, write down the behaviour that they are accountable for. If you find yourself writing generalities, break your expectation into simpler behavioural terms, i.e. what would provide you with evidence that they had done, or not done, what you expected.

3. Write down the specific behaviours that represent your accountability to your own manager. If you find that some of them are not entirely clear, go back to your manager and clarify their expectations.

HUMAN BEHAVIOUR

Seven basic principles of human behaviour that can make your people-management more effective and more ethical.

1. **People like to be free.**
2. **People are accountable for their own behaviour.**
3. **There are consequences for all behaviour.**
4. **People need to know what is expected of them.**
5. **People need to know how they are doing.**
6. **People prefer to own their behaviour.**
7. **Like attracts like.**

People-management is mostly about steering people away from undesirable behaviour, and towards desirable behaviour.

Your efforts to do this will be more successful if you can understand and apply some fundamental principles governing human behaviour.

The principles described in this section are, near enough, universal rules of human behaviour. Although it is possible to identify some abnormal situations where people don't behave in accordance with these principles, the majority of behaviour in the workplace falls within the parameters of the "normal".

Managing people by using and understanding these principles will make the process a whole lot easier than trying to force your way against them. You will also find that using them enhances your image as an effective, fair and humane people-manager, because the things that you do and say will resonate with how people feel they ought to be treated.

The principles set out below are given as if each is self-contained. This is just for ease of presentation.

In practice, they are simply different facets of the one overriding principle:

"Treat people like adult human beings."

After you have read through the explanations of these principles, commit the list to memory so that you can apply them to the planning and implementation of all your people-management interactions.

1. People like to be free

Part of being fully human is the desire to be in control of what we do and what happens to us. The lack of ability to determine what happens in our own lives is one of the biggest causes of stress.

The happiest, most productive people are those who have the freedom to do what they choose, when they choose, and how they choose. This is called "self-actualisation".

Of course, in a civilised society and in any social organisation, there are limits on the extent to which the desire for freedom can be exercised without causing harm to others.

It may help to think of "freedom" as a continuum, with total control at one end and total liberty at the other. Self-actualisation is the process of moving towards the liberty end of the scale.

The most productive organisations are those that can harness this natural desire for self-actualisation in pursuit of collective goals.

However, just because it is a natural tendency, this doesn't mean that you can sit back and let it happen of its own accord. In the context of this principle you have two requirements as a manager of people.

The first is to make sure that you don't do anything to inhibit the self-actualisation process. I'm sure that you have all had experience of (and may even have been responsible for) a working environment in which every detail of every action was documented to the point where there was no room for individual judgement. Of course, there are some aspects of work, such as safety check-lists, which have to be performed in this way, but in most areas of work such a degree of control is unnecessary. It is also counterproductive because it causes people to lose their initiative and enthusiasm.

The second is to make sure you take every opportunity you can to enhance people's self-actualisation. Your role as a people-manager is to enable people to perform to the best of their capability. Ideally, the people who work for you should be doing their job more intelligently and more independently at the end of the year than they were at the beginning.

This will not happen unless, as part of your management process, you make it happen. This is why you are employed as a manager. Your job is to get people to do things which, left to their own devices, they might not do.

So, if you are going to incorporate a feeling of freedom and self-actualisation into your management process, you will not achieve what you want by simply issuing orders and micro-managing at the task level.

We all dislike being **told** what to do or not to do. Among other things, it implies that we cannot decide for ourselves what is the correct thing to do, or that we are incapable of working out how to do it.

When given orders, most people respond reluctantly, unless they have been specifically trained to take orders, e.g. as in the armed forces. When you give orders people may obey, but they will resent your exercise of control. Their resentment often leads them to seek ways of getting their own back. People can be very inventive in their ways of dropping their manager in it. Usually this involves various forms of "working to rule"; doing only the things they are told to do, and nothing else. If they fail to do something, their reason is that they were not specifically told to do it.

It is much more effective if you can arrange for people to **choose** to do the things that you want.

This is not as difficult as it would seem.

You start from the common ground that you are both working towards achieving common goals. These are the goals of the organisation or the team (if they feel unable to accept those overarching goals they can exercise their freedom and leave the organisation).

To achieve those goals, it is necessary to perform actions. Some of those actions are essential. Many are discretionary. Some have to be decided as the task proceeds.

So, instead of saying, "This is what I want you to do," you can achieve what you want by saying something along the lines of:

"This is what I need you to achieve. What ideas have you got? How would you go about it? (Response). That's a good idea. Will you do that?"

By using a technique like this you maximise the person's feeling of freedom and their willingness to perform the task, thus maximising their likelihood of success.

Suggested Practice:

Making things happen in a "free choice" sort of way can be difficult if you are not used to the style. If you want to gain fluency with this style of managing, I would suggest that you write down a few examples of situations where you would

normally just tell someone what to do, and then convert them into a free choice style using any variant of the model above. The examples can be from real life or imaginary, serious or trivial. It helps get accustomed to the technique more quickly if you say the actual words out loud, so you may want to do this somewhere private.

2. People are accountable for their own behaviour

As already described above, "accountable" means that they may be required to give an account (report) of their actions and reasons.

For the purposes of this section we will treat "behaviour" and "performance" as being the same thing, whereas in the rest of the programme they are treated separately as requiring slightly different management techniques.

In its simplest terms, people-management is just behaviour-management.

In other words, the people that you manage have made a commitment to perform certain actions. This is either through the tacit commitment of accepting the job, or subsequently by agreeing to perform specific tasks.

Behaviour consists entirely of things they do, and things they say; nothing else.

As a manager, you want certain behaviours to occur, and others not to occur.

Behaviour is the only thing that you, as a manager, can have any influence upon (you can not directly influence attitude, however much you may suspect that their attitude is "wrong". Attitude is private; you cannot observe what is going on in somebody's head. You may believe that they have a particular attitude, but you can only infer this from their actual observed behaviour). If their behaviour is in some way "wrong", you have a right, and an obligation, to attempt to correct it.

Every piece of behaviour has a reason behind it. Holding people to account involves asking them about their behaviour **and** the reason(s) for it.

As a manager, you are entitled to ask people for details of their behaviour because they are accountable to you. You can only hold them accountable for their behaviour in the workplace. Anything that they do outside of work is none of your business unless it impinges upon their ability to do their work properly, or adversely affects the values of the organisation.

So, the rule, "People are accountable for their behaviour," is more complex than it seems. It really means, "People are accountable **only** for their behaviour." Fortunately, their observed or reported behaviour, plus their explanation, is sufficient material for any of the management interactions covered in this programme.

If people behave the way you want, there is no need for management intervention.

If their behaviour is not what you expect, you are entitled to ask them for an account of their actions and their reasons.

You may also ask them for a description of other people's behaviour, but you cannot legitimately hold them accountable for the acts and omissions of others because they do not have access to the other person's reasons.

As a practical example:

You are the manager of a number of team-leaders. One of the teams has a member who keeps coming in late.

The team leader is **not** accountable for the poor timekeeping of the team member. The **team member**

is accountable to the team-leader for their own behaviour.

The team-leader **is accountable to you** for his/her behaviour, i.e. you can ask them about what action that they have taken to investigate and resolve the problem.

You are **accountable to your manager** for your management of the team-leader.

3. There are consequences for all behaviour

A "consequence" is whatever the person experiences as a result of their behaviour.

Behaviour patterns are established by repeated experience of similar consequences.

A behaviour pattern can be reinforced (strengthened) by experience of consequences that are in some way satisfying or pleasurable.

It can be reduced or extinguished by consequences that are dissatisfying or unpleasant.

In a work situation, the manager provides most of the consequences.

One of your most important roles is to shape people's behaviour in the desired direction by delivering appropriate, timely and consistent consequences.

More information and specific techniques for doing this are given in the section on Consequences.

4. People need to know what behaviour is expected

It is unfair and unproductive to expect people to behave in certain ways unless they are told what the parameters are. A large part of changing people's behaviour consists in getting them to understand what your expectations are.

Telling people your expectations is not the same as telling them what to do.

It does not involve drawing up a long list of rules. This would violate principle 1. It also would take a lot of time; you are bound to miss something out, and it's not the sort of thing you should be doing as a manager anyway.

Some general expectations are set by the job-definition and job-description. These are useful but do not cover every eventuality. Your role as the manager is to provide more detailed interpretation where necessary, and to clarify your own expectations as the need arises.

People need guidelines as this provides them with

the freedom to operate as they see fit within those guidelines.

Without guidelines their motivation, performance and behaviour will stray (usually towards the negative) until they can confirm where the boundary is by stepping over it.

5. People need to know how they are doing

Feedback from other people is an essential component for human development.

This holds true for all aspects of life, but is particularly true in the workplace.

As a manager, your role is to steer people's performance/behaviour away from poor and towards acceptable. When acceptable is achieved, your role is to steer them towards excellent if possible.

We have already looked at the need to set parameters for people generally.

Individuals also need to know how close they are to meeting or exceeding those parameters.

Although most people have the capability to judge for themselves whether they are doing a good job generally or specifically, the reinforcement that they receive from other people helps to keep this capability active.

If they receive no external feedback, their capability is diminished.

6. People prefer to own their own behaviour

People put more enthusiasm and effort into tasks if they "own" the task.

Ownership is part of empowerment, and people who feel empowered work more productively.

The same principle applies when solving problems, even when the problem is of their own making.

In order to maximise the chances of a person actually doing the things needed to resolve a performance or behaviour issue, they need to own those actions.

If you **tell** them what to do to resolve a problem, they will have less commitment than if they **tell themselves**.

This is the reason that all the change-oriented people-management processes in this programme have a step where you ask the person for their own ideas.

The fact that you ask them to implement what you consider to be the best idea does not stop it from being their own idea.

7. Like attracts like

This simply means that if you want the people you manage to show certain characteristics, you have to show them yourself. Their behaviour is affected by your behaviour

If you want them to have confidence in their ability, you need to demonstrate that you are confident in their ability.

Treat people as stupid children and they will behave as stupid children.

Treat them as intelligent adults and they will behave as intelligent adults.

Positive behaviour attracts more positive behaviour.

There may be times when you need to show the appropriate behaviour when you do not genuinely feel it.

This is acting.

In order to be a manager, you have to act as a manager.

Consolidation:

Memorise these principles:

1. People like to be free.
2. People are accountable for their own behaviour.
3. There are consequences for all behaviour.
4. People need to know what is expected of them.
5. People need to know how they are doing.
6. People prefer to own their behaviour.
7. Like attracts like.

Think back over some of your recent management interactions. Can you think of specific things that you said which embodied any of these principles? Can you think of things you said which may have violated these principles?

ESSENTIAL BEHAVIOURAL SKILLS

Each of the management processes described in this book consists of a set of steps. Movement through the steps is made substantially easier by deliberately applying the behavioural skills described in this section.

It might help to think of these skills as the oil that keeps the machine working.

In all people-management meetings you should seek opportunities to incorporate the following skills:

1. Maintain and enhance self-esteem.
2. Listen and respond with empathy.
3. Ask questions to probe for clarity and understanding.
4. Ask for help and ideas to solve a problem.
5. Communicate self-confidence.

In your planning of each interaction, it is helpful to anticipate points in the discussion where these skills are likely to be needed, and give yourself a reminder to use them. It also helps to write down keywords of what you are going to say. Don't rely on your good intention to use these skills, because they are easily forgotten under stress.

Similarly, your notes of the meeting should record your actual use of these skills and the words used.

At first you may feel slightly uncomfortable using these skills in a planned, deliberately formal way. Don't worry about this. All the interactions are planned and formal. When you are conducting a managerial interview you are **acting** as a manager; you are not being your normal self.

It is this difference of style which helps the other person realise that you are operating in "managerial mode", as opposed to just having a conversation in "normal human mode", which you can still do when you want to. You do not have to act as a manager all the time.

So, even if you do initially feel uncomfortable about using these skills as deliberate behaviour, remember that acting as a manager is not about your comfort; it is about obtaining the best results. How you feel about the process is less important than how the other person perceives the process.

1. Maintain and enhance self-esteem

Human beings have a fundamental need for self-esteem; the feeling that they have achieved something worthwhile.

People with sufficient self-esteem tend to put more enthusiasm into what they do.

The largest potential source of self-esteem for most people is their work. Although some people are able to generate their own self-esteem - they know when they have done a good job - it is far more valuable and effective when their self esteem comes from an external source. As their manager, you are that source.

Most of their work-related self-esteem comes from your giving them positive feedback about their achievements.

However, self-esteem can be quite fragile, and there will be many occasions in your people-management where you need to be able to identify lowered self-esteem and take remedial action.

Sometimes the lowered self-esteem may be due to their own perception of failure in not meeting the expected standard of performance or behaviour. Sometimes it will be the result of things that you need to say during the management process. You can anticipate some of this in your planning for the interaction, and you can also "read" the self-esteem levels through the person's body language and general behaviour. Sometimes a low level of self-esteem is a result of their previous experience of being managed.

Each of the processes in this programme requires the person you are managing to leave the meeting feeling positive about their ability to accomplish their commitments.

There are two basic ways of enhancing their self-esteem:

1. Say something positive about what they have achieved.
2. Say something positive about what you think they can achieve.

If you must highlight a negative, ensure that you link it to a positive. When mixing positives and negatives, the wording is very important.

It is crucial to make a distinction between **the person** and **the behaviour**. People feel worse if they think you are criticising them as a person. This is because it is relatively easy to change what you do, whereas it is very difficult to change what you are.

Compare the following:

1. "You are excellent at writing reports but no good at meeting the deadlines." This is heard as "**You ... are no good**".
2. "Your report writing is excellent, and I'd like to get your deadline-keeping to the same standard." This makes it clear that there is a need to tackle the problem of the deadline-keeping and also implies that belief that the deadline-keeping can become excellent.

This effect is primarily achieved by deliberate use of the word "and". Think about what you want to say, and if you would normally use the word "but", try rephrasing it to use "and" instead. The effect can be quite significant.

A person's "pot" of self-esteem is filled, or depleted, by the feedback they receive about things they do in their life.

As their manager you have influence over the self-esteem that they get from their work, which for most people is the largest part of their waking life.

PEOPLE MANAGEMENT #101

Occasionally you will encounter people whose self-esteem has been damaged by their life outside work, or by their previous work experience.

There is little you can or should do about their life outside work. You are their manager, not their counsellor or therapist. However, if you know about their problems outside work, or they tell you during a meeting, it can affect what you need to do as a manager. For example, it might be appropriate to offer compassionate leave, or a rearranged work schedule, or you may need to ensure that they get more work-based self-esteem to compensate for a lack of other sources.

If the person's self-esteem has been damaged by their previous manager(s), this will usually manifest as:

1. Appearing not to care whether they get positive feedback,
2. Seeming to seek negative feedback, or
3. Needing an excessive amount of feedback.

Don't worry about having to "repair" them by giving them excessive doses of self-esteem for ever.

Often you will find that, once they have experienced genuine self-esteem for a while, they will turn their own behaviour round, and become successfully self-motivating.

2. Listen and respond with empathy

There are two elements here.

Listen:

Effective people-management is not about telling people what to do.

It is about stimulating their suggestions and empowering them to do what is needed.

Listening to what they have to say is a vital part of this.

Asking the right questions is an important skill (see next item), but it is even more important to listen to the answers, and to show the other person that you are listening.

In normal conversation you demonstrate that you are listening by using verbal and non-verbal behaviour to indicate that you are paying attention.

In a managerial interview you need to use the same

sort of cues. Sometimes you may need to exaggerate these. It can be a bit like tilting the mirror in your driving test so that you can be seen to be looking in it.

Additionally, you need to do two things which make it different to a normal conversation.

The first is to take notes. This not only provides you with a record for use in subsequent meetings, but also is a very active way of demonstrating that you are listening.

The second is to allow the other person to say whatever they want to say, without contradiction, even though you may disagree with it, or believe it to be incorrect or false. This is particularly difficult when they are saying something which appears to criticise your own managerial behaviour.

The skill of listening is to remember that you have two ears and one mouth. Use them in that ratio.

Respond with empathy:

Note-taking and active listening will enable you to deal with the facts.

Dealing with the feelings and emotions that accompany those facts requires mastery of using empathy. In this programme "empathy" is used in a more precise sense than its everyday usage as interchangeable with "sympathy". Empathy is a specific behavioural technique.

In a normal conversation, the usual response to an expression of feelings or emotion is to contribute a similar one of your own. This is sympathy (literally "suffering together").

Sympathy often has the effect of extending the discussion and leading it away from the original topic. It also implies that you believe that what they are saying is justified.

Empathy is a tool for giving the person a psychologically satisfying response to their expression of emotion, but keeping the discussion on track.

Whereas sympathy says, "I share your emotion (or I can "trump" it with one of my own)", empathy simply says, "I recognise that you have an emotion. I demonstrate that recognition by describing it back to you."

The strange thing about empathy is that your recognition of the emotion is sufficient for the person to feel that you have responded appropriately, and it enables you to move the discussion forward. Sometimes you cannot genuinely use sympathy anyway because you have not had a similar experience, or because you would not feel the same under those circumstances. At least with empathy you can genuinely acknowledge their emotion.

Empathy can be used on both negative and positive emotions, though its effects are not symmetrical.

When used on a negative emotion it "puts brackets" around that emotion and enables you to proceed with the discussion. For example:

"I can see that you're frustrated by the response you've had from Sales. So how else do you think you could get the information?"

Sometimes you can achieve empathy on negative emotions simply by repeating the person's words back to them:

"I see that you feel that this is unfair."

In contrast to the bracketing or dampening effect on negative emotions, when used on a positive emotion, empathy has the effect of amplifying that emotion and boosting self-esteem:

"You must have been pleased with that result."

The essence of "doing empathy" is:

1. Identify the emotion correctly.
2. Put the right name to it.

3. Reflect it back to the person.
4. Move on.

Examples:

1. "I can see that you would find that annoying. Could you think of any way round the problem?"
2. "So you're ok about putting the presentation together, but nervous about addressing a group."
3. "I know that Sam can be difficult to deal with."
4. "So, you are coping on your own. That must be really difficult for you."
5. "So, when others have meetings at their desks you get irritated by the noise."
6. "You must be really pleased about that."

In planning any managerial interaction, anticipate those sections where your questions may generate an emotional response, and prepare your empathy accordingly.

For people-managers, a teaspoon of empathy is more effective than a bucket of sympathy.

3. Ask questions to probe for clarity and understanding

Many of the management interactions involve questioning the other person to obtain details of a problem. This is your right, and your duty as a manager. You are accountable for obtaining their account of their actions

Your role is not necessarily to look for absolute truth. Quite often you will find that people are unwilling to divulge all the facts, and will try to give you a cover story. If you become aware of this, you need to use your judgement about how to proceed. By all means ask further questions if you need to clarify your understanding of their account. The important thing is to capture their account as they wish it to go on the record.

As you proceed with obtaining their account, they may reveal actions which you think were wrong, or just plain stupid. It is important to just record these rather than break out of the questioning phase to engage in criticism. Giving a critical response at this point only makes the person less likely to give you any further information. It also risks turning what should be a problem-solving exercise into an argument.

It follows from the need to avoid criticism that

you should also not use the person's account to allocate blame. Blame should not form any part of your management culture. It is toxic and counter-productive. Of course, things go wrong and people make mistakes. This creates problems; problems need to be solved. Usually, the person that you want to resolve the problem is the same person who created it. They are probably already feeling blameworthy. There is no need for you to add to that negative feeling, particularly when you want them to be positive about putting things right.

When asking questions, it is important to remember that your role is to move things forward by helping the other person identify a solution to the problem. To fulfil this role, you need to know the facts of the situation.

Your actual questions will depend on the situation, but it is helpful to run through a checklist when drawing up your plan for the meeting.

There will obviously be some questions specific to your work environment, but the standard set of What, Who, When, Where, How and Why, will guide the majority of your initial questions and further probing.

What?

"What happened?"

"What have you done about it so far?"

"What did he/she say/do?"

Who?

"Who did you speak to?"

"Who else was involved?"

When?

"When did this happen – what time?"

"When did you first notice...?"

Where?

"Where were you?"

"Where did this happen?"

How?

"How did he respond?"

Why?

Sometimes you can't avoid the question "Why?" However, before you go ahead with "Why" it is worth considering whether you could get the same information (or better) by rephrasing your question.

There are two reasons for this:

1. "Why?" can sometimes sound antagonistic or critical.

2. "Why" can be ambiguous. For example, if I say "Why do think he said that?" am I questioning your motive or his?

It is preferable to use the phrase "What is the reason...?"

If I ask "Why were you not at the meeting?" this implies that I think you were wrong not to attend the meeting.

If I ask "What is the reason you were not at the meeting?" this says that I believe everything you do has a reason (you are an adult), and I need to know what your reason was.

Finally, remember that you will usually need to ask follow up questions to gain more understanding before you can help people to solve their problems. You need to gain information about how they actually go about their work.

The more expert you become at people-management, the less you will be involved in the fine detail of how people go about their daily tasks.

It is a strange paradox that while most workers prefer their work not to be closely supervised and inspected by their manager, they still expect their manager to know everything.

Skilful planning and use of questions will help you maintain an overall understanding of what they do, so that you can delve into the detail when necessary. In this way you can reinforce your credibility as a manager.

4. Ask for help and ideas to solve problems

It is very motivating and empowering for a person to feel that their manager values their input to solving a problem.

It boosts their self-esteem to be treated as an adult who has valuable expertise.

Use a phrase such as, "So, I now understand the problem. I'd like to know what you think could resolve it. What ideas can you suggest?"

Even when the problem being addressed is one of their own making, they are still the expert at solving it.

In contrast, being told what to do undermines their self-esteem and makes them feel they are being treated as a child.

Many managers have become managers on the basis of their technical problem-solving skills, and find it difficult to refrain from simply telling the person what to do and how to do it, because this takes them back into the comfort zone of success in their previous job. Although this might appear to be quicker, in fact it takes longer. When you tell someone what to do, you also have to "sell" the idea if you want it done effectively. When they generate their own ideas they have already done the selling to themselves.

Asking people for help in solving a problem provides a range of benefits:

Short term benefits:

1. It produces an immediate boost to self-esteem and motivation.
2. It develops a stronger commitment to implementing ideas they have generated.
3. It taps into detailed job knowledge unavailable to the manager.

Medium term benefits:

1. It creates a more collaborative manager/staff relationship.
2. It reduces any tendency to delegate upwards, and reminds you not to seek upward delegation
3. It helps identify development needs.

Long term benefits:

1. It changes the organisation's culture, and makes people more positive in their commitment.
2. It changes people's perception of management.

5. Communicate self-confidence

This skill is about **your** self-confidence that you can help the other person solve **their** problem. By demonstrating that you have confidence in your management process you also convey the message that you have confidence in the other person's capability. This is not as difficult as it may sound, because the techniques of this programme cover every aspect of people-management, and each process will produce a positive outcome if you follow the steps.

Of course, there will be occasions when you do not feel fully confident in yourself or in them. No matter what you may **feel**, it is necessary to **behave** as if you are confident in your ability to reach a positive outcome to any people-management situation. Sometimes acting as a manager literally does involve acting. Noel Coward was once asked, "What is the secret of good acting?" and responded, "Just say the lines, and don't trip over the furniture."

Even if you have to pretend at first, after a few

sessions your successful experience will make your confidence genuine.

It helps if you approach each interaction with the following hierarchy in mind:

1. This is a problem that needs to be solved.
2. I am confident that you can solve it.
3. If you can't solve it, you and I can find a solution for you.
4. If you and I can't solve it, maybe someone else can help.
5. If no-one can solve it, it is insoluble.
6. If it is not soluble it is not a problem, it is a feature.

You also need to give this self-confidence to the other person.

Many of the management meeting structures in this programme include a final stage of conveying to the other person your confidence through your verbal behaviour. There are two reasons for this:

1. The reminder ensures that you have a written record of being supportive if your managerial style is subsequently criticised.
2. It gives the person an additional boost and ends the meeting on a positive note.

Consolidation:

Memorise this list of skills:

1. Maintain and enhance self-esteem. (SE)
2. Listen and respond with empathy. (E)
3. Ask questions to probe for clarity and understanding. (P)
4. Ask for help and ideas to solve a problem. (AH)
5. Communicate self-confidence. (SC)

Now that you are sensitised to the need for these skills, study other people's interactions (television soaps are a good source) and note down any examples using the suggested abbreviations. Also try to note down the actual words and context so that you could describe the example to someone else, as this is good practice for your note-taking skills.

CONSEQUENCES

In its simplest form, people-management is concerned with taking action to encourage desired behaviour and to discourage undesirable behaviour. Among behavioural psychologists this is known as Operant Conditioning.

Any trained psychologists among you will soon recognise that what is presented here is a gross simplification of the results of decades of scientific research, and I may be slightly loose in my use of terms which have precise scientific meanings. My response would have to be that I am not in the business of training psychologists; I am in the business of training managers.

You don't need to fully understand the workings of a car in order to drive. Similarly, you don't need a full understanding of behavioural psychology in order to gain a benefit from using basic Operant Conditioning; a general understanding of the principles will suffice.

Another issue which I must also address at the outset is the question of morality. The techniques of Operant Conditioning are commonly used for training animals, and some may feel that in using these techniques the manager would be acting as if their staff were nothing more than laboratory subjects. My response would be that the morality depends on what the techniques are used for.

It would be possible to train a human to dribble when a bell rings, as Pavlov famously did with his dog, but it would be a pointless thing for a manager to spend their time on. There are far more meaningful behaviours that need to be addressed in the people-management environment. Also, it should be remembered that the "lab rats" have chosen to work in this environment, and have thus agreed to adhere to certain forms of behaviour which are regarded as worthwhile in their own right.

A further moral concern that some may have is that, on the whole, people may not be aware that their behaviour is being shaped by the use of psychological techniques. Is it legitimate to manipulate them in this way? My answer would be that we all do it all the time, albeit unwittingly. If somebody holds a door open for you and you smile and thank them, they become more likely to continue holding doors for people. If you scowl at them they become slightly less likely to hold the door open for the next person.

So, assuming that the techniques are used in accordance with basic human dignity, and for agreed worthwhile ends, there should be no problem about using Operant Conditioning. The only problem is how to use it effectively.

The general principle of Operant Conditioning is that behaviour associated with a **reward** tends to recur, and behaviour associated with a **punishment** tends to decrease.

In the people-management context the use of the terms "reward/punishment" can be misleading. Many managers interpret "reward" as meaning more money, and for various reasons, there is little, if anything, they can do to manipulate the pay or bonus system as a tool for shaping behaviour within the timescale required for effective management.

The most effective reward and punishment that a manager can deploy is their own behaviour, and for the most part this is verbal behaviour.

That is to say, a piece of managerial behaviour which makes a person feel good will be perceived as a reward, and a piece of behaviour that makes the person feel bad or uncomfortable will be perceived as a punishment.

In other words, people's behaviour is shaped by the consequences of their actions. You, as the manager, are the person who ensures that the right kind of consequence happens.

There are three types of consequence:

Positive:

Positive consequences are those perceived as pleasant by the receiver. These have the effect of stimulating more of that type of behaviour in an effort to receive more of that consequence.

Negative:

Negative consequences are those perceived by the receiver as unpleasant. These have the effect of reducing or extinguishing that type of behaviour in order to avoid further unpleasant experience.

Neutral/Zero:

Neutral or Zero consequences are those where a consequence might have been expected, but nothing actually happens. The effect of neutral consequences depends on many factors. In general, what tends to happen is an increase in consequence-seeking behaviour.

If the appropriate consequence was negative, i.e. a punishment for unacceptable behaviour, when nothing happens the behaviour will continue and escalate. For example, a few instances of arriving late to work will soon become a habit if no remedial action is taken.

When good behaviour fails to yield a positive consequence, the person will eventually seek negative consequences by changing their behaviour to the unacceptable. This is most commonly seen in parenting, when a child's attention-seeking behaviour is not acknowledged. The behaviour moves more and more towards the unacceptable end of the scale until it provokes a reaction.

Adults' behaviour is more sophisticated, but works on the same principle.

The application of consequences is a very powerful tool. It is worth bearing mind for your people-management strategy that some of the people you manage may have had experience of incorrectly applied consequences, i.e. negative or zero consequences applied to laudable behaviour, and positive or zero consequences experienced in connection with poor behaviour.

Applying consequences

1. In order to be effective, a consequence must be associated closely in time with the behaviour. Immediate is good. Soon is ok. Late is worthless. For example, if you give someone praise for doing good work today, it will help shape their behaviour. The same praise in six months' time will have no effect on shaping their behaviour.
2. The consequence must be associated with the specific behaviour. That is to say, the person needs to be given a clear understanding of the reason that they are receiving a positive or negative consequence. So you need to make it clear which behaviour you are reinforcing.
3. It is usually necessary to supply a consequence several times in order to establish the association.
4. Individuals vary on how much reinforcement they need, and how often.

Initially your "reinforcement schedule" may need to be quite frequent; you may need to apply reinforcement to every instance of the behaviour. Later you can reduce the frequency and still maintain the effectiveness. In fact, an intermittent reinforcement schedule amplifies the effectiveness of the consequence in controlling behaviour. Slot-machine manufacturers have this down to a fine art. They calculate the optimum frequency of payouts to maximise the behaviour of inserting coins.

The great advantage of using consequences to shape workplace behaviour is that it is a reward system which does not cost you anything.

People-management is mostly based on verbal behaviour, so you can create appropriate consequences by your choice of words.

Although this programme is designed to provide guidance when you are managing people in formal situations, you can also use consequences to shape people's behaviour when you are interacting informally.

When you see any sign of the behaviour that you want to encourage, then a little bit of positive reinforcement such as "Good job", "Well done", or, "That's what I like to see", will have significant effect. I have talked with a lot of managers who think that they already give sufficient positive feedback to the people they manage, and see no need to do more. When I talk to their staff, most cannot recall any specific instance of positive reinforcement.

Bear in mind; it's not about whether **you** think it is sufficient, it's about whether **they** think it is.

This informal use of positive reinforcement can often save you a great deal of work later, though, of course, you should also use the opportunities for positive reinforcement contained in the formal management processes in this programme.

Negative reinforcement for poor performance or behaviour needs more careful thought.

All reinforcement should be directed at the behaviour, not the person.

If you get this wrong with positive reinforcement it doesn't matter too much because the person will just get a boost of self-esteem instead.

If you get it wrong with negative reinforcement, e.g. an emotional outburst directed at the person, they will experience it as an attack on them as a person rather than their behaviour. This will make them defensive and less likely to co-operate in finding a solution.

If you feel you must express an emotion it is better to describe it than to demonstrate it.

"I am annoyed/disappointed (with the performance/ behaviour/ results)."

The majority of your reinforcement should be based on positive consequences for positive behaviour, because most of your management activity should focus on getting people to do more of the good things rather than less of the bad things.

It is up to you to define what counts as positive behaviour. If you concentrate on a narrow band of behaviour such as hitting sales targets, you will miss out on all the other facets of people's capability which could contribute to the long term wellbeing of the organisation and its individual members.

Remember that managing people is managing individuals. There is no "One size fits all".

Your delivery of consequences has to be adapted to the developmental needs of each person.

Your aim should be to have a better team of people at the end of the year than you started the year with.

Consolidation:

Think of some specific examples of desirable workplace behaviour. What kind of consequence could you administer in order to maintain and enhance that behaviour?

Think of some examples of poor workplace behaviour. Imagine, or recall, the type of consequences which may have reinforced this

behaviour.

Set yourself a daily target for the number of times you should say something positive and encouraging.

NOTE TAKING

Templates for the planning and conduct of all the management meetings are obtainable free of charge from: www.reflextraining.co.uk.

From now onwards, almost all your people-management will take place in structured face-to-face meetings. This does not mean that every time you talk to someone it has to be in "manager mode". It is important for you, and the people you manage, to be able to distinguish between a normal person to person interaction and a managerial interview.

Every time you have a managerial interview with anybody, it is important to take notes for the following reasons:

1. It demonstrates that you are listening, particularly if you check back with the other person to ensure that your notes are correct.
2. It gives you time to think; the paper that you write your notes on can also contain your plan, so you can check whether you have done enough to move

on to the next step.

3. It gives you control of the direction and pace of the interaction.
4. It makes people less likely to lie to you. A verbal lie can always be denied or re-interpreted. A lie that is written down is on the record forever.
5. It makes the other person more likely to fulfil their commitments if they know that you have written down and checked what they said they would do.
6. It makes it easier to monitor subsequent progress. You will be managing a number of different people, and each will have different strands of performance/behaviour that you are seeking to influence. Unless you have total recall, you are not going to be able to remember who should have achieved what and when.
7. You need an accurate record in order to give an account of the managerial actions you have taken.

Many managers are put off the idea of taking notes because:

1. They think note-taking involves recording every word that is said. This is clearly impossible while having a meaningful interaction.
2. They don't plan their interactions, so they have no

idea where the discussion is going to lead.

Taking notes is **not** the same as making a transcript. If you want a record of every word spoken, you might as well use a recording device. Bear in mind that while electronic recording might appear to save time and effort during the meeting, the post-meeting effort of processing the data outweighs any benefit.

Obviously the main purpose of interview notes is to provide a **sufficient** record of the **relevant** parts of the interview.

This record is for your use only, so it only needs to contain sufficient information to trigger your memory at a later date. This means that you can use whatever forms of shorthand or abbreviations make sense to you.

As you become more accustomed to using the techniques in this programme you will find that your speed and accuracy of note-taking will increase such that your making notes become a natural part of your interaction and will not interfere with the pace of the discussion.

The essential components of the record are:

Participant names

Date

Time

Type of discussion

Reason for the discussion

Questions and answers

Commitments given

Timescale for actions

Date of next meeting

Note-taking becomes less of a chore if you split it up into things to do **before**, **during** and **after** the interview.

Before:

The "administrative" parts of the record are known before the meeting takes place. So you don't need to waste the other person's time by using the first part of the meeting to record these details. This would also be counter-productive because it makes the tone of the meeting appear more formal than it should.

Similarly, if you have planned the main questions and subsidiaries that you intend to ask, then the main bulk of your note-taking is already done.

It is also useful to identify sections of the meeting where you intend to increase the effectiveness of the interview by using specific people-management skills. For example, you may plan to express disappointment at the person's achievements. Although this will be directed at the performance, not at the person, they will still experience it as criticism. If you know this, and want to make them more positive in suggesting solutions, you could plan to boost their self-esteem by praising some other aspect of their performance. Your notes could include shorthand cues to apply the appropriate skills. You can just tick these off as the meeting proceeds.

During:

If you have prepared your "script" in keyword form, all you now need to do during the meeting is jot down keywords to encapsulate their responses and suggestions.

Many managers find it useful to write planned questions on the left of the paper so that they can tick off the questions as they are used and note the response next to them. You usually do not need to write down their every word. Just a few key words should be sufficient to recall the gist of what they said.

Wring down the responses gives you the control of the meeting, gives the impression that you are really listening to what the person has to say, and enables you to get the facts straight.

You check the facts by summarising your notes back to the person with phrases like, "Let me just check that I've got this right; you say the reason this happened is…"

You may feel at first that working to a structure from prepared notes, and taking time to write further notes, makes the process a bit stilted and mechanical. Don't worry about this; you will become more "fluid" with practice. Anyway, people expect a management interaction to be somehow different from a normal interaction, and the note-based approach conveys the message that you are treating the issue seriously.

After:

You may find that the notes you have made before and during the interview are sufficient to serve as a record as they stand. If so just add them to your file, and note the next meeting in your diary. Add any action commitments that you have made to your "do-list". If you are doing people-management on a number of people, you will probably need to keep a management file on each person. This is not their personnel record; it is for your use only.

Many of the processes in this people-management suite require more than one meeting to resolve issues.

The test of your notes is, "Will I be able to make sense of all this the next time I meet this person?" If not, then a bit of time spent tidying up the notes will pay dividends.

Remember, your interview notes are just a tool to help you manage more effectively. They have no other purpose.

At the next meeting you will be able quote what was said by each of you, and what commitments were made, so that you can check progress.

If all goes well you will probably never need the notes again. However, you should not get rid of them in case your management style and actions are later called into question. Claims for unfair dismissal or constructive dismissal often hinge upon allegations about what the person's manager said or did (or didn't say or do). While having accurate notes will not guarantee refutation of the claim, being able to quote what was said, and when, will certainly give you a stronger defence. Also, the knowledge that accurate records exist may forestall some clams.

Consolidation:

The only way to develop speed and accuracy is practice and more practice. A useful way to start is with recordings of conversations from television. Take a few sheets of paper and draw a line down the middle. Write the names of the people at the top of each column. As each person speaks, capture what you can in the appropriate column. Take notes of the conversation in real time using whatever abbreviations, short-hand, symbols and squiggles you think may help. Run the recording back. Check the comprehensiveness and accuracy of your notes.

In time you will be able to capture not only the words but also the participants' reactions. This will provide you with useful information on how words can affect behaviour.

Templates for the planning and conduct of all the management meetings are obtainable free of charge from: www.reflextraining.co.uk.

PLANNING

Templates for the planning and conduct of all the management meetings are obtainable free of charge from: www.reflextraining.co.uk.

Creating, implementing, monitoring and reviewing plans, is the largest part of every manager's job.

Managers have two main aspects to their job; the technical and the human.

No manager who wishes to keep their job would dream of trying to run the technical side without a plan.

Any good plan should include the following:

1. Objectives

A simple statement of the desired outcome, preferably conforming to the SMART criteria which state that objectives should be **Specific, Measurable, Achievable, Realistic, Time-related.**

2. Milestones

While objectives tell you where you want to get to, Milestones give you information about whether you are still on the right path, and how far you have progressed.

3. Deliverables

Deliverables tell you what tangible outputs will be produced during, and on completion of the plan.

4. Timetable

This should include target time, elapsed time, and contingency.

5. Accountabilities

Not just a general description of responsibility, but a clear statement of what actions are to be performed, and by whom.

6. Issues

Any unknowns or problems that need to be resolved before the plan can be successfully executed.

Not many managers put this amount of effort into planning the human side of their job. This is absurd because 80% of most managers' objectives are actually achieved by other people. Many, in fact, do not plan their people-management at all, preferring to rely on their gut-reaction and emotion when faced with a people-problem.

While it may not be necessary to plan each people-management interaction to the same level of detail as a technical project, some basic planning is essential to ensure a positive outcome.

Every management interaction must be based on a plan. This does not mean that every time you open your mouth you have to be operating under a plan. In this system of people-management there is still room for normal human banter and chit-chat. What it does mean is that every time you decide to go into "manager mode" you must have a plan.

In preparing your plan, the following questions will help you focus on your strategy and tactics:

What is the situation that I am concerned about?

Is it something that I can live with, or is it something that requires managerial intervention?

What are my accountabilities in this situation? The easiest way of answering this question is to think, "If my manager asks me what I have **done** so far to resolve the issue, what would I like to be able to say?"

Which people-management process is the right one to use?

Mostly, the appropriate technique is fairly self-evident. You might occasionally have a difficulty deciding between Delegation (which is about passing over some of your own accountability) and Introducing Change (which, among other things, is the process to use when you are just allocating a task).

What do I know about the background?

What do I know about this person?

What is their job, age, general approach to work, accountabilities, any other relevant details?

What are the circumstances leading up to this interview?

Is this the first time this issue has been raised, or is it part of a continuing process?

What is the factual evidence? You can only manage a person's behaviour – things they do or say (or omissions of behaviour). You cannot manage their attitude. Changing people's behaviour often does seem to change their attitude, but there is no way of verifying this.

What outcome do I want?

This is where you set your objective(s). This is easier to clarify if you outline it in behavioural terms; what do you want the person to do?

What questions do I need to ask?

Think about your main, and subsidiary, questions.

Also think about how you will phrase those questions in order to appear assertive but not aggressive.

How is the person likely to react?

Given that you want the interaction to generate a positive behavioural outcome, which of the people-handling skills will you need to use at each step in the interview?

Initially, this depth of preparation will take you some time, and you may not get it absolutely right the first few times. Any planning is better than none. Failing to plan is planning to fail.

PEOPLE MANAGEMENT #101

Once you have had some practice, you will find that you can plan quite swiftly, particularly if you are using a printed template of the interview steps for planning and note-taking.

Do remember, however, that the process of constructing the plan is performed "off-line", i.e. you are not under pressure. You have the space to explore a range of options. When you actually implement the plan in a face-to-face meeting you are doing it in real-time and under a bit of stress. A plan that is too detailed will cause you to stumble because you won't be able to see all the detail when under pressure. A plan that is too sketchy will leave you with embarrassing gaps where you have to think about what to do or say next.

The ideal plan contains just sufficient detail and key-words to guide you from one step to the next. Only through practice can you find the level of detail that suits you. Ideally you should rehearse your plan with somebody else. This will enable you to find out whether you can actually say the intended words, and you can gain some feedback on whether the words achieve the intended effect.

Failing that, at least run through the structure in your head, but say your words out loud. If you find that you can't say the words as planned then you either need a bit more practice, or some different words.

Templates for the planning and conduct of all the management meetings are obtainable free of charge from: www.reflextraining.co.uk.

THE TECHNIQUES

If you have read this far, you now have all the information and skills you need for application to specific types of people-management interaction.

Although every people-management meeting you conduct will be unique due to the organisational background, the particular situation, and the people involved, the **type** of meeting will be one of the ten classic structures below.

Each structure is designed so that, if you follow it, you will achieve the desired outcome in the shortest possible time.

The desired outcome is usually a commitment on the other person's part to undertake some form of behaviour that they would not otherwise have done.

A secondary outcome, though still a very important one, is that conducting meetings within these structures generates a feeling on the other person's part that they have been well managed. This has the result of making them more inclined to fulfil their commitments. The continued positive experience of being well managed has a significant effect on their future behaviour and performance; they become more capable of managing themselves.

Each type of meeting is designed to produce a positive outcome. This does not mean that one meeting will resolve all your management issues. Sometimes you will need to have a series of meetings with an individual to tackle one issue. Individuals are complex, as is their behaviour in a work situation. Sometimes you will need to address multiple issues with the same person. Often you will find you want to talk to a person who is performing well in some areas of their job, and has significant development needs in others.

It is vital for success in using these techniques to make it clear to yourself, and the person you are managing, that each meeting deals with one topic only. You cannot manage every aspect of a person's work at once. If you contaminate a discussion with details that should be dealt with in other types of meeting you will undermine your original purpose.

Failure to separate the different "threads" in your management of a person will, at the very least, mean that your meetings take longer than they need to. At worst, the meeting could actually reverse any progress that you have made with the person.

You should also bear in mind that although the primary purpose of these meetings is to manage employees, they can also be used, either as they stand or with minor adaptation, for managing other relationships such as suppliers, customers, indirect reports, other managers. Although they can often be quite effective in "managing" adolescents, I would strongly recommend that you avoid any attempt to use them on a spouse or partner.

The types of people-management meeting covered in the text are as follows:

1. Delegation
2. Reviewing Progress
3. Introducing Change
4. Responding to Concerns or Complaints
5. Giving Praise or Recognition
6. Managing Performance
7. Managing Behaviour
8. Taking Follow-up Action
9. Disciplinary Action
10. Dismissal.

These are presented in two sections. The first section (Meetings 1 – 5) details those meetings which should occupy most of your time. They are the sort of things that you need to do when everything is going smoothly, and you want to keep it going smoothly. Delegation and Reviewing Progress obviously go together. The others are more stand-alone techniques to be used as and when necessary.

The second section (Meetings 6 – 10) contains the ones that you need to use when things are not going right. They are all designed on the principle that it is better to cure the problem rather than replace the person (even if only because it is cheaper) and so each technique is designed to produce a positive outcome.

However, a positive outcome may not always be the result, so the separate techniques are also structured on their escalating degree of seriousness, culminating in dismissal as a last resort. If it ever gets to this stage, dismissal **is** a positive outcome of sorts.

DELEGATION

Steps of the process:

1. Describe specifically your expectations.
2. Explain the reasons your expectations are important.
3. Ask for help/ideas for achieving the expected results.
4. Discuss each idea and express your support.
5. Decide and record specific actions and timing. Set follow up date.
6. Express your confidence in the person to achieve the expectations.

If you wish to progress as a manager, your primary task is to make yourself redundant. That is to say, after a suitable period in your current role you should have created a situation in which everything that you are accountable for can be achieved by somebody else in your team.

Some managers take the opposite approach and construct an environment where their presence and participation is essential to the success of every activity. These managers may be seeking to convince themselves and others that their value lies in their indispensability, but this is a very short-sighted way of doing things.

The end result of keeping all your accountabilities to yourself is that the capability of your team members is under-utilised and under-developed. You will not feel confident about leaving them to get on with things in your absence, and they will be no more competent in their job at the end of the year than they were at the beginning. In fact, they will probably be less competent because they will have got into the habit of referring back to you for every minor decision.

So, if you would like to spend some time away from the office without frantic phone calls, or take a stress-free holiday, or develop your career, delegation is the key to your success.

Delegation might better be described as **establishing accountability for results**, because this more accurately identifies that it is a more complex process than just telling (or, preferably, asking) someone to do something. Delegation is the process for handing over part of your management accountability to someone else. It is not just the process of handing out tasks. If you simply want to allocate a task that a person already knows how to do, you should use the steps in the chapter "Introducing Change".

As a manager, about 80% of the work that produces "your" results should be performed by other people. When you reach 80% and everybody knows what to do, how to do it, and can do it to the right standard you can safely take time out (for holidays, sickness, conferences, or spend more time working on strategy) with confidence that everyone will get on with what they are meant to do. When you reach 100%, it is time to make your next career move.

Sadly, most managers are nowhere near achieving the 80% target.

Many managers spend most of their time on micro-management; allocating and monitoring individual tasks, technical problem-solving, or even doing the tasks that should belong to others.

Their motto is: "If you want it done right you've got to do it yourself". Although they "delegate" by handing out tasks that they would prefer not to do, or have not got the time for, they remain in close contact with the performance of the task, ready to take over when necessary.

Some managers avoid delegation because they fear losing control of the results, or fear that others might be more successful.

Others don't delegate simply because they are not sure how to do it effectively.

The process described below is for those managers who want to be able to use an effective technique for delegating.

Like all the management processes in this programme it is presented as a sequence of steps designed to be easy to learn, easy to follow, and achieves the end result in the most effective and efficient way possible.

Proper delegation involves selecting an area of the results that you are accountable for, giving that accountability to the other person, and managing their achievement of the results.

If delegation is done properly the person taking on the accountability undergoes a developmental experience which makes them more valuable to you and the organisation. To put it more simply: One of your accountabilities as a manager is to ensure that your team becomes measurably more competent over time.

1. Describe specifically your expectations:

As with all the techniques described in this book, you need to make it clear at the outset of the session what the topic of this particular meeting is intended to be. The purpose of this is to differentiate it from any of the other topics that you might address with this person on other occasions.

You will need to use your judgement about how much, if anything, you tell the person about the subject of the meeting beforehand. If you give them a brief outline of your intention before the meeting, some people will use the intervening time to thinking about how they would achieve what you want, thus potentially saving considerable time on the discussion. Others may spend their time thinking only of the difficulties.

You can eliminate confusion and uncertainty about where this meeting is going by stating precisely one or two specific behaviours (results) that you expect. The level of detail needed will vary from person to person depending on their skills, experience and job-maturity. Remember to describe your expected results rather than the specific tasks needed to achieve those results.

You have selected this person to take on some extra accountability because you believe that they are currently capable of doing it, or that they will be able to learn how to do it within an acceptable timescale. They may not fully share your confidence, so in addition to identifying the specific outcomes required, you may need to boost the person's self esteem by stating the reason that you have selected them.

For example:

"The new machine is arriving next month. I appreciated your help in producing the work procedures for the current machine, so now I'd like you to take on the production of an operating procedure for the new machine and train all the team to use it within a week from installation."

As opposed to:

"The new machine is arriving next month. It's going to be your responsibility to ensure that it is used properly."

By opening the meeting with a statement of the specific results needed, you ensure that the rest of the meeting is about how (not whether) to achieve those results.

2. Explain the reasons your expectations are important

There are two reasons for taking the time to do this:

1. It enhances the person's self-esteem and motivation to succeed.
2. It provides an opportunity to explain to the person how their performance fits in to the "bigger picture". This is often a neglected area in people-management, but it is vital for motivation. People's motivation and performance declines when they do not have a clear understanding of how their work contributes to that of others. Although you may understand how all the bits fit together it is not safe to assume that everybody else does.

There are usually three areas where the importance of the results can be identified. These are:

1. Importance to you, in terms of your meeting your objectives. Contrary to popular opinion, most people in most organisations do want to be helpful, or be perceived as helpful to their manager. Although some of this is attributable to simple career-development motives, much of it is an innate human tendency.

2. Importance to the person for their career-development, expansion of their skill-set, reputation etc. Rather than trying to sell this idea to someone who is comfortable with their current workload and skill-set, it is better to set the tone that continual development of their capability is something that you expect.
3. Importance to the work group. The "work group" may range in size from the immediate team up to the whole company, if appropriate.

Even if you are sure that the other person understands and shares your view of the importance of what you are asking them to do, say it anyway. It does no harm, and can do a lot of good. Sometimes it is necessary for a manager to act a little dumb, and state the blindingly obvious. Remember that this is a management interaction, not a normal human interaction. People expect you to act differently when being a manager. In a normal human interaction, you can go back to being a normal human.

3. Ask for help/ideas for achieving the expected results

This is where the interaction transforms into a two-way discussion. Use a phrase like, "So, I need your help to make this happen. How do you think you could go about it?"

There may be a need for the person to clarify your expectations, so allow this to happen, and then focus the discussion on how the expectations are to be met.

Although it may be tempting to state your own ideas for them to achieve what you want, it is important to allow the other person to come up with their own ideas. These may even turn out to be better than yours, but the point is that people only feel ownership when they participate in creating their objectives.

Although you may think you know how the person should proceed, you must not dictate your ideas to them, otherwise you are not really delegating you are simply giving them a list of tasks.

The person's commitment and participation is necessary for them to be successful. You will undermine this if you do not allow them to put forward their own ideas.

You may, if necessary, plant ideas on the person

with phrases such as:

"Have you considered...?",

"How would you feel about doing...?"

Take notes of whatever ideas they suggest. You may use subsidiary questions to clarify what they mean, but it is important not to start analysing in detail before their set of ideas is complete. There are two reasons for exercising restraint:

1. There is a risk that you both get so involved in analysing one idea that you become bogged down in detail, to the exclusion of other ideas.
2. If you analyse the first idea and find that it won't work, the person has received a negative consequence for generating that idea, and so is less likely to generate further ideas.

Once a reasonable set of ideas has been brought out, you can then move the meeting to the next stage.

4. Discuss each idea and express your support

Discuss the other person's ideas first, not necessarily in the same order that they were given.

Then, if necessary, offer your thoughts.

This is the stage of the discussion where specific actions start to be identified, so you can both be more analytical.

As in all parts of this process, you may need to hold yourself back from being too "helpful". Remember that delegation is not just about relieving your workload; it is mainly about giving the other person an opportunity to grow their skills.

You are not necessarily looking for a completely well-formed outcome, but the likelihood is that they will generate a reasonable set of ideas. It is ok if they are unclear about some of the detail of what they should do, so long as the next step identifies this or gives them an action like, "Think about it, and come back to me to discuss how you think you would want to do it."

There may also be times when, although you know the solution, it may be more important to leave them to struggle a little as a necessary learning experience. If you do this, make sure that you pick up the issue at your next meeting to check whether they have learned what they needed to.

Your support may be necessary in order to overcome some obstacles beyond the other person's control. Also you may identify a need for training or coaching before some of the ideas can be implemented.

Once you have discussed the set of ideas, they still do not "belong" to anybody until you complete the next step.

5. Decide and record specific actions and timing. Set follow up date

You are unlikely to be able to remember precisely what the person said they would do unless you write it down. The same goes for any actions that you may have committed to. The meetings that follow this one are going to be either a Progress Review or a Performance Management. Your starting point for either of these is an examination of the commitments that each of you made.

Be very precise in the wording of who is going to do what.

Use "You" and "I" to identify ownership of particular actions. Some managers like to use phrases such as, "We need to ensure that...", thinking that this makes it feel less like an order. Wherever possible, avoid the use of "we", because it maximises the possibility of confusion about who will actually perform the action.

You will need to set follow up dates. Do not assume that once you have had this discussion, everything will proceed smoothly to the outcome. Delegation involves a learning/developmental process, so it is likely that you will need some interim checks to see how things are going, or whether some unforeseen difficulties have emerged.

Setting follow up date(s) establishes a sense of priority and demonstrates that you are serious.

It is most likely that you would use the follow-up date(s) for a progress review, though other processes may also be appropriate.

Ensure that follow-up dates are in your diaries, and go to the final step.

6. Express your confidence in the person to achieve the expectations

You may feel that this should go without saying, but remember, nobody really knows what you think. They can only interpret your behaviour – the actual words that you say.

You want the person to feel confident about achieving your expectations. If you tell them that you are confident, some of that confidence will be transferred.

Leaving out this step can cause damage. Putting it in does no harm, and can do a lot of good.

When you have completed all these steps, which should not take very long, you will be confident that you have done everything you can to maximise the person's likelihood of success. You can safely leave them to get on with it on their own, knowing that they cannot go too far astray because of the built-in checkpoints, and you may even be pleasantly surprised that they do it better than you would have.

Consolidation:

Memorise the sequence of steps:

1. **Describe specifically your expectations.**
2. **Explain the reasons your expectations are important.**
3. **Ask for help/ideas for achieving the expected results.**
4. **Discuss each idea and express your support.**

5. Decide and record specific actions and timing. Set follow up date.
6. Express your confidence in the person to achieve the expectations.

Using the process template, make a plan for the following situation.

You have been spending too much time resolving technical problems particularly those whose solutions involve external expenditure. You have a team member who is just as capable as yourself at identifying problem solutions but who refers these issues to you because they have no spending authority. You wish to give this person the ability to authorise external expenditure up to a specific limit, and thus make them the first point of reference for technical queries from their colleagues.

Plan carefully what you would say in the first two steps. Particularly make it clear what you want the person to do (in behavioural terms). Consider also what you may need to say to boost the person's self-confidence.

Anticipate the other person's responses, both technical and emotional, and plan your responses accordingly.

Construct a realistic set of actions for each of you. Consider what kinds of monitoring and reporting mechanisms will need to be in place, at least for the early stages of the handover.

Now rehearse the meeting, saying all your planned words out loud and not forgetting step 6.

Repeat the whole exercise using an example from your own environment.

REVIEWING PROGRESS

Steps of the process:

1. Review your expectations and ask for progress.
2. Probe for both achievements and problems.
3. Listen actively and respond with empathy.
4. Compliment the achievements; summarise problems identified.
5. Ask for and discuss ideas to solve the problems identified.
6. Decide and record specific actions and timing; set a follow up date.

When you have delegated an area of accountability, or a task, correctly you should have the confidence to let the person get on with the work without interference.

This does not mean that you just abandon the person and await the result.

An important part of the delegation process is setting up a progress review date for the person to report on their achievements.

There are four main reasons for holding a progress review:

1. It is an important source of information. The more successful you become as a people-manager, the less time you will have to spend on close monitoring of people's day to day achievements. This is a good thing, because it conveys a message of trust. However, you do need to be kept informed about successes and failures in case your assistance is needed to resolve any issues. It also helps you keep an overview of the reality of the workplace without being perceived as interfering.

2. It communicates the importance of your expectations. People have plenty of other things to do in addition to the specific area that you are currently interested in. Unless you remind them of the importance of this one by having a meeting focused solely on this one topic, they are likely to move it down their personal priority list.

3. It is an opportunity to reinforce progress. Often when you delegate, the person is doing this type of

work for the first time. Their progress may not be as much as you would expect of a more experienced person. Any progress is better than none. Making the person feel good about what they have achieved so far boosts their motivation to achieve the remainder.

4. It identifies problems and their possible solutions. If it emerges that the person has not made as much progress as you would have liked, it could well be that you or they have underestimated the difficulty of achieving the agreed outcome. One common reaction when people encounter a problem is that they try to delegate upwards. A weak manager will, as a result of flattery or out of desperation, take over accountability for resolving the problem. Eventually such a manager will take back all the work, and then complain about being stressed. The message you should convey is, "It's ok to have problems; they go with the job you undertook. I'm here to support you in working out a way to solve your problems."

Conducting a progress review in the following sequence is the most effective way of ensuring a positive outcome to the meeting in the shortest possible time, and further progress on the achievement(s). Additionally, once people have got used to this style of interaction, they will tend to come into the meeting with their proposed solutions already thought out. This will save you even more time and effort.

1. Review your expectations and ask for progress

This simple opening sets the tone for the meeting. It should be neutral and factual. You may already have some information from other sources about how they are getting on. There is nothing to be gained, and some trust to be lost, if you mention this.

For example: "Last week you took over production of the stats for the quarterly report, and you said that by today you'd have made some progress on a draft. So how has it gone so far?"

The simple opening tells the person that the sole topic of this conversation is progress on that specific task, and that you are not currently interested in any of the other topics that you may be addressing in other meetings. As your people-management activity increases you will have several ongoing "threads" with each person. The rule for optimum effectiveness is to keep these threads separate. One meeting equals one thread. If you mix them together, you will undermine the effectiveness of each process.

Opening the discussion in this way also tells them that you have not pre-judged what they are going to say. It says: "All progress is good. I trust you to give me an honest account. If you haven't made the amount of progress that you expected, then there has to be a reason."

This maximises the likelihood of the person participating positively and productively in the meeting.

Once you have clarified the purpose of the meeting, proceed to the next step.

2. Probe for both achievements and problems

At this stage you are only probing for the facts about what they have accomplished and what obstacles or problems they have been experiencing. Where necessary, seek clarification and understanding by using follow-up questions on the details.

Your questioning should be focused solely on gaining a clear understanding of the achievements, the non-achievements, and the actions which led to these outcomes.

It is likely that you will get simple descriptions of positive achievements, but more analytical description of reasons for non-achievement, because people will always seek to avoid blame. If, by using these people-management techniques you have created a blame-free environment, they will still want to go into more detail on the "failures" in order to help you to help them to find a solution.

Things that you must not do during this probing are:

1. Expressing any negative emotion about any lack of progress, because this will tend to inhibit the person from being open and honest with you. Also, you may not yet have been told their reason for the lack of progress. It is unfair, and it undermines your managerial status, to criticise with no evidence.
2. Analysing problems and starting to look for, or imposing, solutions. You will have an opportunity for collective analysis later. At this stage, premature problem-solving will take the meeting off track, and is likely to cause you to overlook other important issues. It will also make the meeting take longer than it should.

Just probe for clarity and write down their answers.

3. Listen actively and respond with empathy

Although you, as the manager, can ensure that you do not express emotion about what the person is telling you, they may not have the same degree of control. They may express positive emotions about what they have achieved, or negative emotions (disappointment, frustration, annoyance etc) about what they have failed to achieve.

You will obviously be noting down the facts as they emerge and demonstrating your eagerness to ensure accuracy by reflecting them back to the person. It is just as important to take note of feelings or emotions expressed, and demonstrate your understanding by using empathy.

Empathy, as opposed to sympathy, will provide a satisfactory response and enable the meeting to proceed more positively.

At this stage you are more concerned with collecting the facts. Analysing the facts comes later.

4. Compliment the achievements; summarise problems identified

What you are doing at this stage is putting together the whole picture from the individual pieces gathered at the earlier stages.

Put all the positive achievements together, and give some praise or a compliment, then move on to give a summary of what remains to be achieved, or problems that need to be overcome.

This enables the next part of the discussion to focus solely on the negatives, but in a positive frame of mind.

5. Ask for and discuss ideas to solve the problems identified

Of course, if the progress has totally met your expectations, and there are no problems identified, skip this step and go to step 6.

The main emphasis at this stage is to get the other person to generate ideas for solving the problems that they have identified. Your role is supportive in enabling them to do this.

As in all the management processes where you seek the input of the other person, you direct the discussion by your questioning, summarising and note-taking. The primary objective is to get the person to generate their own solutions, so it is important to refrain from analysing individual suggestions until there are no more suggestions forthcoming. This avoids potentially putting a negative cast on the discussion by spending time on an idea which turns out to be a "non-runner". The procedure is "Ask, note, ask, note... discuss."

It is quite possible that some of the solutions proposed may require action(s) from you. Sometimes this is legitimate because your intervention **as a manager** will enable the person to make better progress. In other cases, it might just be a ploy to get you to take some, or all, of the task back. This can be tempting especially if you know that you could actually perform the task(s) quicker or more effectively than the person they now belong to. If you fall into this trap it is not good for your long-term achievements or your stress levels because you end up doing their job in addition to your own. Also it is not good for the development of the other person if you allow them to pass up the opportunity to learn how to resolve problems for themselves.

Then you can move to the final step.

6. Decide and record specific actions and timing; set a follow up date

This is where you take back control of the meeting by stating, and recording, what specific actions are to be taken, when and by whom.

This is not dictating or giving orders. It is simply selecting from a range of suggestions already discussed.

The act of writing it down with timings just turns it from an intention into a commitment.

Set a date in your diaries for the next meeting. The next meeting is likely to be a further progress review or a review of the final results.

Consolidation:

Memorise the sequence of steps:

1. **Review your expectations and ask for progress.**
2. **Probe for both achievements and problems.**
3. **Listen actively and respond with empathy.**
4. **Compliment the achievements; summarise problems identified.**
5. **Ask for and discuss ideas to solve the problems identified.**

6. Decide and record specific actions and timing; set a follow up date.

If you have not already done so, go back to people who are working on tasks for you and fix a date and time for an interim review meeting. Use the planning template to prepare for the meeting. Pay particular attention to the wording of your questions. While you need to elicit enough information to determine whether corrective action is required, you do not wish to appear aggressive or critical. Prepare to respond positively to reported achievements. Prepare to respond neutrally to any lack of achievement. Your role is not to criticise underachievement but to help the person find a way to get over their problems.

GIVING PRAISE OR RECOGNITION

Steps of the process:

1. Describe specifically the improvement or achievement.
2. Explain the reason this is important to you and others.
3. Listen and respond with empathy.
4. Provide the appropriate form of praise or recognition.
5. Sincerely thank the person.

Given that people work better if they feel positive about their achievements and abilities, it is a good idea to take every available opportunity to praise them or thank them for the good work that they have done.

Given also that this is so obvious, you may be wondering why I make mention of it. Sadly, in my experience, there are many environments where managers fail to exercise this basic courtesy, or they believe that they give sufficient positive feedback when in fact the people they manage perceive a distinct lack of it.

When you give praise or recognition on a regular basis it is usually informal, and so does not count as a specific management technique. You do not need to plan your tactics, although you might need to make a resolution to praise people more often, and measure how well you keep that resolution.

The praise and recognition techniques described below are in a different league from everyday courtesy. They are a powerful management tool.

It is easy for people to become accustomed to regular praise such that they probably have a general feeling of wellbeing but would find it difficult to recall any single specific piece of praise and the reasons for it.

In contrast, when people experience a structured management interaction devoted solely to praise or recognition, they tend to remember it for a very long time and the effect on their motivation is very significant.

It is a very powerful technique, so it should be planned as carefully as every other management process, and used sparingly only when the situation requires it.

The particular situations where you should use a structured praise/recognition meeting are:

1. When you have previously been counselling somebody about their performance/behaviour, and they have shown a satisfactory improvement. You would use this process to give an intensive positive reinforcement to the change, to maximise the chances of the improvement becoming permanent.
2. When somebody has done something above and beyond what you would reasonably expect. You probably will not be able to reward this type of action with extra money, but you certainly want to encourage more of that type of behaviour. This type of immediate, intensive praise costs nothing, and is actually more effective.
3. When you feel that a steady, reliable worker is in need of some recognition. This is more difficult to remember to do. On the whole, steady reliable workers tend to exhibit less need for recognition than the other two categories, and can often be taken for granted by their manager. However, they do still need some, otherwise their steadiness and reliability will tend to decrease.

The technique is designed primarily for use with individuals, but may be easily adapted for use with groups. For example, you could use it to praise a whole team for their efforts, or for giving an award as part of a public ceremony.

You will need to use your discretion about whether to conduct a praise and recognition session in private or in public.

The general rule of people-management is "criticise in private, praise in public".

There are some benefits to public praise; it spreads the message that you value certain forms of behaviour, and can encourage others to emulate the achievements of the person being praised. It also enhances your public image as a competent people-manager.

However, if you are praising someone for making an improvement to their behaviour or performance, it may not be tactful to let everyone know what base-line the behaviour or performance has improved from.

One practical advantage of praising someone in public, usually at their workplace, is that it gives you control over the ending of the meeting.

This interaction is very short (a couple of minutes),

and in order for it to be fully effective you need to ensure that it consists of the process steps and nothing else. If you go out to the other person, you can relatively easily terminate the interaction by going back to your office. If the person is already in your office, it may feel slightly uncomfortable that the interaction has been so short and you both may be tempted to start discussing other things.

It is important to ensure that the meeting is not "contaminated" and its effectiveness reduced by having other topics mixed in with it.

1. Describe specifically the improvement or achievement

You know the reason you initiated this meeting. The other person, initially, does not. It is important to make it clear to the person as soon as possible what this interaction is going to be about.

No matter how effective you become as a manager, people will always feel slightly nervous when called to a meeting and they don't know what it is about. In order for them to get the full force of this process you need to put them at their ease.

As you become more experienced in this style of management the need to differentiate one type of meeting from another becomes more imperative because you manage people along several threads simultaneously. As an extreme example, you may be involved in disciplinary action on one aspect of their performance/behaviour, and at the same time need to give them praise for improvement on a different thread.

So, a generic model for your opening gambit should be something like:

"Since we last spoke about X you have done Y and Z."

The person needs to know right from the start **exactly** what it is that you are pleased about. Then they can quite reasonably assume that this meeting is not going to be uncomfortable.

Avoid vague phrases like, "You've made a lot of progress," unless you can back that up with specific examples of what you mean by "progress".

2. Explain the reason this is important to you and others

Even by this stage they may not be entirely at ease, because past experience might have led them to believe that a statement about their achievement will soon be followed by a big "but".

Explaining the reason that you value their achievement makes it clear that the interaction is going in a pleasant direction. This emphasises the value of what the person has done and makes the praise more effective.

It also helps the person understand how their contribution contributes to the bigger picture thus helping to create a feeling of belonging, or reducing the feeling of, "My boss never tells me what's going on."

You may think people share your understanding of how their work helps and supports others. This is not a safe assumption. For many people, the last time they were given "the big picture" was at their induction.

Even if you feel that they do understand the effect of their contribution to your targets, team productivity or morale, it does no harm to tell them. It adds to the "warm glow" that you are seeking to create.

3. Listen and respond with empathy

Up to this point you have driven the interaction, and the other person has said nothing.

Now that you have told them that they have done something that you value, you give them a chance to respond.

PEOPLE MANAGEMENT #101

People tend to react to their manager obviously heading towards praise in one of three ways:

1. Total surprise.
2. Modesty – "Oh it was nothing really. I was just doing my job."
3. They try to tell you how difficult the achievement was.

Empathy is the appropriate response in all cases.

1. "I can see I've taken you by surprise, but I'm sure you're as pleased as I am."
2. "Well I'm glad you see your job in that way." However tempting it may be, **do not** make any negative reference to other people who may not be as praiseworthy. The whole tone of this interaction has to be positive.
3. "Yes I know you overcame a lot of problems." Breaking off to discuss what those problems were devalues the whole process. Do not undermine the force of the praise by analysing the problems or discussing any negative issues. Book a later session if need be.

The empathy acknowledges their feelings and enables you to move to the next step of actually giving the praise.

4. Provide the appropriate form of praise or recognition

You may feel that by telling them that you are pleased you have given them sufficient recognition. They may not share that feeling, so it is important to give them something that makes it absolutely clear.

This may be a simple "Thank you," or, further recognition such as telling them that you are putting a note in their file, or a commendation. In other cases, it may involve the presentation of a token of reward.

In planning for this interaction it is helpful to keep the first steps descriptive and factual, and keep the actual thanks/recognition for this step, so that you don't become self-conscious about praising the person now, when you have already done it earlier.

You should also plan to avoid "contaminating" the praise/recognition with anything else.

The classical "contaminants" are:

Extra work or additional accountabilities. Quite often a person's achievements indicate that they are capable of expanding their role. If you have this in mind, do not discuss it here, otherwise your praise will be interpreted as a cynical ploy. Even if the other person starts pushing for extra tasks or career enhancement, do not branch out into discussing the issue. Just use empathy, and arrange to discuss it a later date.

Discussion of financial reward. If the person raises the question of financial reward you will need to be encouraging, but non-committal:

"It's good that you are keen to develop your career. Pay increases and bonuses are decided on an annual basis, and achievements like this count towards the decision."

5. Sincerely thank the person

If the recognition involved some sort of token, such as a badge, a tie, a certificate etc. or a "mention in dispatches", then add your personal thanks.

If "Thank you", was the only appropriate reward, this step is simply a reminder to check that you have actually said it. Many managers find it difficult to actually say the words.

Do not assume that just because you are doing a

process called "praise/recognition" the other person will feel praised or recognised. The words "Thank you," must be said.

If you have conducted this interaction at the other person's workplace, you can end it simply by going back to your own work.

If you have called the other person to your workplace, you will need to give a clear signal that the interaction is over.

If the person has mentioned issues that will need further discussion, make an appointment for a later date. It is important to let the person have some time to experience the warm glow, i.e. the positive feeling of having received praise/recognition. Any further discussion of any topic at this point will reduce that positive feeling and reduce the effectiveness of your action.

Consolidation:

Memorise the sequence of steps:

1. **Describe specifically the improvement or achievement.**
2. **Explain the reason this is important to you and others.**

3. Listen and respond with empathy.
4. Provide the appropriate form of praise or recognition.
5. Sincerely thank the person.

Identify someone in your environment who deserves praise or recognition. Use the process template to plan the interaction. Rehearse the interaction out loud.

INTRODUCING CHANGE

Steps of the process:

1. **Provide background information. Explain the reasons for the change.**
2. **Describe the change and its effects, both positive and negative.**
3. **Ask for questions about the change. Respond with facts and empathy.**
4. **Commit to providing further information. Set follow up date.**
5. **Ask for help to make the change work.**

There are two aspects to your position as a manager; the maintenance role and the development role. The maintenance role is to keep things working smoothly. Mainly, you achieve this by managing the performance and behaviour of the individuals in your team to ensure that standards are met and maintained.

The development role involves making

improvements to the way people and processes work.

As a manager you are frequently making changes. Sometimes these are local changes which you initiate. At other times you introduce larger changes on behalf of other managers.

With local changes, for example, those affecting individual work practices or the introduction of new equipment it is always advisable to consult the experts, (i.e. the people in the workplace) beforehand. They are experts in their own job, and are highly likely to identify issues that you may not have thought of. The consultation process also helps to pre-sell the proposed change, making acceptance easier to achieve.

When introducing larger changes, again transparency in the decision-making process makes it easier to gain acceptance of change, though sometimes you will have to forego this for reasons of information security.

Whatever process you use to decide what the change is going to be, you will have to accept that there is the possibility of a negative reaction when you tell people about the change. This is a natural reaction because change moves people from the known into the unknown. On the whole, people prefer to stick with what they know. Reactions will range from slight caution to outright hostility.

If you can reduce the negativity by prior consultation you will find that introduction of the change will be easier, and acceptance will be quicker.

This set of steps will enable you to convert any residual resistance into acceptance and support.

Throughout this process, the emphasis is on avoiding the question of **whether** to implement the change and concentrating on **how** to implement it.

Usually you will find that people who initially resisted a change adapt quite happily to it after a short while.

This set of steps can be used when announcing change to a group, as well as to individuals. If necessary, you can also use this format for breaking bad news.

1. Provide background information. Explain the reasons for the change

The acceptance of change, with minimal resistance, is determined by the extent to which people perceive the change as necessary.

It is always helpful to take any opportunity you can to give people information about "the bigger picture".

In this process, the background information prepares them mentally for the topic of the meeting so that the actual announcement of the change is less surprising.

Even when you believe that they already know the background, it does no harm to give a summary.

This provides you with a reasonably comfortable way of opening the meeting rather than jumping straight in with the announcement.

A phrase such as, "As you may be aware... This means that it is necessary to..." lets you describe the general background which has led to the need for change and the more detailed causes for the actions you are about to describe.

Now that you have prepared for the announcement of a change, you give the detail.

2. Describe the change and its effects, both positive and negative

You need to ensure that there is no scope for discussion of what the change(s) will be, so at this stage you need a clear and precise statement of what will happen, and when.

Using an opening statement like "So what this

means is that from next Monday onwards you will..."

Many managers make the mistake of only describing the positive effects of a change.

Of course, no-one will introduce a change in order to make things worse. But enthusiasm for the benefits of the change can sometimes blind you to the negative effects that others will inevitably perceive.

People will doubt your intelligence or your integrity if you try to "sell" a change by mentioning only the good points. Demonstrating that you have thought about how others may perceive a downside to the change will help forestall or disarm some potential objections.

So, a "good news, bad news" approach is what you need. You should, however, avoid the use of the terms "good" and "bad", because they are your interpretation. Often you will find that people respond the opposite of what you expected. Simply describe the full range of effects, and leave it to others to make their own judgement.

In cases where you are introducing a change as an improvement, the positives should outweigh the negatives, otherwise there would be no point doing it in the first place.

In other cases, you may be telling them of a

change which is all, or mostly, bad news; where the negatives outweigh the positives.

In both cases just state the effects neutrally.

The overall purpose of this set of steps is to make it clear to people exactly what they need to do to make the change happen.

3. Ask for questions about the change. Respond with facts and empathy

Essentially this step should focus on **how** to implement the change, not **whether**.

The purpose of this step is to let the other person work out the details of what it will be like when they are implementing the change.

When they imagine themselves in the position of doing it, they are "buying" the idea, so you don't need to do so much "selling".

Dispose of emotional reactions by using empathy, and keep the discussion to questions of fact.

If the change has been fully thought through, you should be prepared to answer most of their questions, and you will find that most apparent "objections" are actually requests for more detail, or suggestions for improvement.

If you find any questions that you cannot answer; thank the person, and make a note of the question.

If the questioning involves seeking your views, and you are actually not enthusiastic about the change, be careful how you deal with this. It is not legitimate to say, "I think this is a bad idea but the Board says it has to be done." It is legitimate to say, "The majority of the board voted in favour of this. The decision has been made, and I will implement it."

When there are no further questions, move on.

4. Commit to providing further information. Set follow up date

This step may not be necessary if you have satisfactorily answered all the questions.

If there were questions that you could not answer, undertake to come back with the information by a specific date.

Similarly, if you have had requests for additional information that will help the implementation, e.g. lists, schedules etc. give your commitment to provide this.

You may also wish to set a review date to ensure that the change is actually implemented, and to gain feedback on any unforeseen difficulties.

5. Ask for help to make the change work.

All you have done so far is to announce the change and discuss ways they can make it work. This is perilously close to telling them what to do. You now need to obtain the person's commitment to implement it, so that there is no doubt about their knowing that the change has to be implemented.

So, as a final step, say something like:

"I need your help to make this work. Will you do it?"

If you have completed all the previous steps, there can only be one answer, which, of course, is, "Yes." Beware of "I'll try," this really means, "Probably not."

Consolidation:

Memorise the sequence of steps:

1. **Provide background information. Explain the reasons for the change.**
2. **Describe the change and its effects, both positive and negative.**
3. **Ask for questions about the change. Respond with facts and empathy.**
4. **Commit to providing further information. Set follow up date.**

5. Ask for help to make the change work

Use the process template to prepare how you would announce the following:

A. Your team works in an open plan office. Some people have been eating their lunch at their desk instead of in the staff room provided. This sometimes leaves an aroma which is objectionable to other staff and is noticeable to visitors. You are now introducing a company-wide policy that all meals must be consumed away from the office area. Decide whether to announce this change to the group collectively or on an individual basis. Anticipate the range of reactions and questions that you are likely to get.

B. Your organisation has just secured a lucrative contract with a company that is very security conscious. The customer insists that all documents relating to the contracted work be subject to tight security procedures. You are about to brief the leader of the team who will be carrying out the work. You know that some of the most creative workers in the team have a very informal approach to document control and will find the new procedures (signature for release of each document, clean desk policy, no documents to leave the premises) a significant change from their usual way of operating.

RESPONDING TO CONCERNS OR COMPLAINTS

Steps of the process:

1. **Listen intently and respond with empathy.**
2. **Probe for facts and possible corrective actions. Take notes.**
3. **Summarise your understanding.**
4. **Provide factual information, personal experience, and your position.**
5. **Clarify specific actions. Set follow up date.**
6. **Thank the person for bringing the concern or complaint to you.**

Although this process is mainly designed to handle concerns or complaints from staff, its structure is also an effective model for handling colleagues, senior managers, customers and suppliers.

This is one of the few situations where the driving force behind the interaction comes from the other person, not from you. This means that you cannot plan the details of the interaction in advance because you do not know until you have started the process what the subject of the discussion is going to be.

Nevertheless, you can have your general handling strategy learned and prepared beforehand so that you can drive the interaction towards a positive outcome, thus enhancing your image as an effective people-manager.

However, a few words of caution are necessary here.

Many people become managers because in their previous job they demonstrated expertise in solving problems. Solving problems demonstrated their usefulness to the organisation and provided them with their main source of self-esteem. When they are promoted, they often have difficulty cutting back on this role, and indeed, many go out of their way to become embroiled in problem-solving instead of concentrating on being a manager. Taken to extremes, such "managers" find themselves continually fire-fighting or operating in crisis-management mode; and secretly they love it because it gives them the self-esteem that they may not yet be getting from being a proper manager.

So, if you adopt a style of management which encourages people to bring you all their problems, they will do just that. You will have a sense of accomplishment, but your people will gradually lose confidence in their own capability. If you doubt this, I once heard a senior Team-Leader ask his boss whether he should use a drawing-pin or blue-tack to stick up a notice. Fortunately, the manager was a recent replacement for a very hands-on predecessor, and he responded appropriately with, "Which would **you** like to use?"

As a competent people-manager, you want your team members to be willing to make decisions within the parameters of their accountabilities, and to resolve their own problems when they can. As you move up the managerial ladder you become less involved in the details of how people work. Like it or not, you need people to be able to sort out technical issues and interpersonal problems for themselves. They are the experts now; not you. Or to put it more simply, the whole point about being a manager of people is that **your job** is to get other people to do **their job**.

As you apply the set of techniques in this programme, your people will progressively become better at doing their job, eventually reaching the point where they can do it without your involvement at all.

Don't worry about that. When you reach that point it simply means that you are ready for the next rung in the ladder, i.e. being a manager of managers.

The strategy below will enable you to encourage and develop autonomy in your team members so that they don't feel they have to pass every decision upwards. They will pay back your efforts by behaving in a far more adult and productive way.

On the other hand, you don't want to make them feel that they cannot ask for your input at all, because there will be some occasions when they genuinely need your help or advice. If they can't get what they need from you the problem may fester, or they may go over your head, which is not good for your reputation.

So this technique involves a balance. You want to discourage people from coming to you with issues that they ought to tackle themselves, but you also want them to feel that they can come to you with the right sort of problems.

If you are fully into the role of people-manager it is less likely that people will be coming to you for help in solving technical problems.

The issues that they bring up are more likely to be sensitive people-problems, often relating to the workplace behaviour of others.

1. Listen intently and respond with empathy

The purpose of this interaction is not necessarily to resolve the problem immediately, but to make the person feel that they have been handled correctly. Often you will find that handling the person correctly makes the problem go away. The person just wanted to blow off some steam.

Quite often, the other person's verbal and non-verbal behaviour will indicate how serious or urgent they feel the problem to be. Ironically, the downside of being an effective people-manager is that your people become more empowered to resolve their own problems without needing to refer to you. This means that when someone does feel a need to refer to you the problem or issue is likely to be more serious or urgent.

So, no matter what you are doing you should pay attention to their immediate need. Your concentration on whatever you were doing has been broken anyway, so you might as well pay attention to the interruption.

Your first action has to be to show that you are listening. Use phrases like, "I can see that you are annoyed about something. Sit down and tell me what's on your mind."

This will enable you to find out:

1. What the specific issue is. More precise information comes later, but at least you will find out what **type** of problem it is.
2. How serious or urgent the issue is to the person. This may not be the same as its seriousness or urgency to you.
3. What they feel about the issue. Feelings are likely to be concern, worry, anger, frustration. Using empathy to reflect the emotion back, helps overcome the emotion so that the problem can be tackled more calmly.
4. How much of your time it is likely to take.

Only then are you in a position to offer them options about how to proceed.

If the problem is genuinely urgent, you have little choice but to stop whatever you were doing and follow through with the rest of the process.

In many cases, though, people convey a sense of urgency because they are not aware of your work schedule and availability.

It can be quite acceptable to say, "I can give you five minutes now, or I have a free half hour this afternoon. Which do you think you'll need?"

Assuming that you decide to have the meeting now, proceed to the next step.

2. Probe for facts and possible corrective actions. Take notes

At this stage you only know that there is a problem. You have no idea of the details, or of what needs to be done (or even whether anything can/should be done).

Quite often people feel the need to build up a head of steam before they raise an issue with their manager. The result of this is either:

1. They present a simplified version of the issue. Often their opening gambit is an ultimatum, or a request/demand that you do something; e.g. "I can't work with Sam any longer." Or, "Something has to be done about people parking in the disabled spaces."
2. They describe small elements of a problem without identifying the main problem.

Your probing questions will help you lead them into a frame of mind which gets them away from their feelings and onto the facts.

The other effect of asking probing questions is that it makes the person have to work to convince you that there is something to be concerned about.

"So, what did he actually say?"

"What do you think is causing this?"

"What do you think would resolve the problem?"

"What have you done about it so far?"

"How often has this happened?"

"Is anyone else affected?"

This helps you to keep a balance between being approachable, and being inundated with trivia. You need to convey the impression that you are willing to help resolve the problem so long as they can convince you that there is a need to do so.

Make it clear that you are listening for the facts by writing what the person says, including the feelings that they express.

3. Summarise your understanding

This is not just a ploy. You need to ensure that you really have understood their concern or complaint.

Additionally, you need to demonstrate that you understand it from the other person's point of view.

You may need to return to step 2. for clarification.

Use your notes to provide a summary of the facts, including facts about feelings expressed, and move on.

4. Provide factual information, personal experience, and your position

You don't need to do all of these things. They are options. You will need to select according to the circumstances.

In relation to the examples above:

"The things you described are not like Sam's normal behaviour. Before I take it any further I'd like you to talk with Sam and have a go at resolving your differences. If that doesn't work, please come back to me."

"Nobody but genuine badge holders should park in those spaces. The main culprits have been identified and reported to their manager."

Provide factual information about relevant company policies or background information relevant to the issue that the complainant may be unaware of.

"A memo about parking regulations will be issued to all users next week."

You also need to tell the person your position; i.e.

what type of action you believe is necessary as a result of their raising the concern or complaint.

Sometimes the type of action you, the other person (or both of you) need to take will be obvious.

In other cases, particularly when the concern or complaint is about a third party, it would be wise to get the other side of the story.

If you have relevant personal experience of a similar situation, particularly one which was resolved successfully, you can use this to show that you are taking the issue seriously. It also gives credibility to actions that you prescribe at the next step.

5. Clarify specific actions. Set follow up date

Specific actions will depend on the nature of the concern or complaint.

Wherever possible, the aim in this step is to pass accountability for resolving the issue back to the other person.

Your questioning at step 2 may have identified some actions that they have not yet tried.

If appropriate gain their commitment to perform those actions so that you can review their success or failure at your next meeting. The next meeting will follow the structure of a Progress Review.

In some cases, the person's current skills may not be sufficient to resolve the issue. Rather than automatically taking accountability for resolving the problem yourself, or giving them a set of instructions on how to resolve it, consider the option of coaching. You could show them how to do Performance or Behaviour–Management. You could give them a copy of this book and help them practice the techniques in a separate session.

In many cases, there will be specific actions for each of you. The concern or complaint may have revealed a system failure that can only be cleared by managerial action, or it may simply be that you need to talk with other people and gain more understanding of the situation before committing to a specific action.

Make it clear what you will do and what you need them to do, and set a date for a Progress Review.

6. Thank the person for bringing the concern or complaint to you

This is not just a courtesy, although being polite and courteous in the workplace is a good thing to do anyway.

By thanking the person, you are saying a number of things:

"You have done the right thing." This is particularly necessary when the complaint has been about another person's behaviour. Most adults retain a strong memory of "playground rules", and find it uncomfortable to report on others

"Thank you for bringing it to **me** rather than to someone else."

"Thank you for letting me know that something I thought was ok, actually is not."

"Thank you for bringing it to me before it got any worse."

By regular use of all the six steps in this process you will find that you have to cope with fewer crises, either because they are resolved before needing your intervention, or because you will have become adept at turning a **crisis** into just a **problem**.

Problem solving is far less stressful than crisis-management.

Consolidation:

Memorise the sequence of steps:

1. Listen intently and respond with empathy.
2. Probe for facts and possible corrective actions. Take notes.
3. Summarise your understanding.
4. Provide factual information, personal experience, and your position.
5. Clarify specific actions. Set follow up date.
6. Thank the person for bringing the concern or complaint to you.

Worked example:

Consider the following situation. On Monday a team member comes to you insisting that you change the work rota so that they don't have to work the skeleton shift on the coming Saturday. After your probing questions you are told the reason is that his son is playing in his school football final on that day. The team member has known about the rota for a month but only learned on Friday that the boy had been selected for the first team after another boy became ill. His relationship with his son has been difficult recently, and he feels that showing his support is essential to help show he cares.

The team member is a good worker and you don't want to be perceived as the person who prevented him supporting his son. You could just say "Leave it with me," and then spend several hours trying to find someone else who is willing to do the shift. On the other hand, you do not have time to do this, and it is not really your job anyway. You need to encourage people to resolve their own problems.

You need to empathise with the difficulty of his situation but also need to make it clear that he is accountable for covering the shift. However, since all team members are capable of doing the Saturday work, your position is that you would have no problem if he were able to arrange a swap with one of his team mates.

His actions will be to find a team mate willing to swap, and to let you know who his replacement will be. Your actions will be to swap the names if he is successful, and to inform the payroll department.

If he succeeds, you will have enhanced your reputation as a benign but assertive manager. If he fails, then he knows that you also would have

failed, so he cannot hold you responsible for his missing the match.

By the way, did you notice that I just told you how to tell the complainant how to resolve his problem? Can you think of a way of handling this so that the complainant generates the idea of an informal swap for himself?

It would be nice if your entire experience of people-management consisted of Delegation, Progress Review and Giving Praise or Recognition, but life is not always like that.

The theme for the next group of processes is, "What to do when things are going wrong."

Sometimes people's performance or behaviour deteriorates below acceptable standards, and you have to take action to help them get back to doing the job correctly.

Sometimes, as a new manager, you inherit chronic poor performance/behaviour and need to undo the effect of their previous experience of being managed.

Sometimes the process of turning things around can be achieved quite quickly. At other times you may need to engage in a structured sequence of meetings in order to reach the desired positive outcome.

The sequence is as follows:

Performance Management or Behaviour Management:

The outcome of each of these meetings is a positive commitment to take action to remedy the problem. If it works with just one application, then you would use a **Praise & Recognition** meeting to reinforce the change.

If the desired change does not materialise, there can only be three reasons:

1. The action has not been taken.
2. The action has been taken, but did not cure the problem.
3. The cause of the problem is more complex than you were told, and needs further analysis.

Use your judgement about whether to repeat the Performance or Behaviour Management process, or to escalate to:

Follow Up:

In a Follow Up meeting you again approach the problem seeking a positive commitment to implement another solution or to ensure implementation of the original commitment. A Follow Up meeting reinforces the message that the management process will not stop until the problem is resolved. If it works, you use a **Praise & Recognition** meeting to reinforce the change, otherwise you move on to:

Disciplinary Action:

By this stage you are less interested in the reasons that they give, and more insistent that change is necessary. Sometimes people need to get to this stage before they realise the seriousness of not changing. You gain their positive commitment to make the desired change, and if it works you use a **Praise & Recognition** meeting, or you move on to:

Dismissal:

In which the positive outcome is the termination of a relationship which is obviously not working and not repairable.

PERFORMANCE MANAGEMENT

Steps of the process:

1. **Describe specifically the problem.**
2. **Probe for causes. Note answers. Summarise for completeness and understanding.**
3. **Ask the person for help to solve the problem.**
4. **Ask for and note possible solutions. Evaluate suggestions.**
5. **Decide and note specific actions.**
6. **Set date and time for follow-up.**

If you examine the HR literature about performance management you will find lots of inspiring articles explaining that it is a good thing for staff and managers to work together on the achievement of a set of agreed goals. This is all good, high-level strategic stuff. I have no argument with that principle. If you seek something more tactical, however, the only practical technique ever offered is Performance Appraisal.

Having worked with many appraisal systems, and even having designed a few, I have come to the conclusion that they are tools for addressing a different issue than the day-to-day management of individual performance. Well-designed appraisal systems can be a useful mechanism for assessing the capability and development needs of an organisation. They can also be used to simplify the distribution of rewards, though this usually engenders such a degree of suspicion and manipulation as to render the whole process worthless.

An appraisal is usually too far removed in time from the actual performance to have any value other than as a historical record. It cannot help you, as a manager, to do anything about today's performance. You need to be able to do something about current under-performance a long time before the appraisal and, with a bit of skill, help the person improve their performance before it impacts upon your team's results.

Even though your achievements as a manager depend on other people's performance, you are not accountable for their individual performance (they are). You are accountable for your team's overall performance, and for your own actions to rectify any performance problems.

You may have people in your team who occasionally, or consistently, put in a performance which is below the standard that you expect. As a manager it is your job to hold people accountable for their own actions and omissions (i.e. to ask them for an account of what they did or did not do, together with their reasons).

Your own manager can quite reasonably hold you to account for the actions that you take when the team's overall performance is at risk from individual members' underachievement

You are accountable to your manager for the actions you take in order to raise performance to an acceptable level, and to exceed that level wherever possible. Your manager has a right to ask you for your account of what you have done:

1. To ensure that team members know what performance you expect.
2. To measure performance so that you can find out whether it is meeting/exceeding/falling below your expectations (obviously, the measures by

which you evaluate performance will be specific to your industry and particular circumstances, so are not covered in this programme).
3. To reinforce and maintain satisfactory/excellent performance.
4. To investigate reasons for under-performance.
5. To assist people to remedy their under-performance.

The focus of this process is on what you need to do when you find that an individual's performance is below the standard expected. Incidentally, if your organisation does use an appraisal system, you will find that the technique described below will make your life easier because your description of performance over the appraisal period will consist largely of the summaries of the individual people-management interactions, which you will have in your notes.

When things are going right, the job of the manager is easy. It is when things are not right that you might feel that you have to brace yourself for a difficult or unpleasant discussion.

Fortunately, it is not going to be as difficult as you might think, so long as you remember to approach it as a joint problem-solving exercise rather than an opportunity to give negative criticism.

Nobody sets out initially to do a job badly. On the whole, people like being able to meet or exceed their manager's expectations. When people know that they are working well, their feeling of self-esteem creates a positive feedback loop which enhances their overall performance and well-being.

In contrast, when they are failing to achieve the results that are expected, they feel bad. The classical technique of putting in extra effort to make them feel even worse is actually counterproductive. While such an outburst may temporarily diminish the manager's anger or frustration, it does nothing to remedy the problem and can provoke unhelpful behaviour.

Your role as a manager is to help them identify the reason(s) for the problem, and assist them to overcome it.

You need to approach inadequate performance as a joint problem-solving exercise.

You need to conduct it in a positive, supportive way so that the person overcomes their negative feelings and starts to feel good about getting their performance back on track.

This technique is designed to be positive and assertive while boosting the person's desire to succeed in meeting your expectations.

1. Describe specifically the problem (using documented evidence, not feelings)

Your opening description needs to be evidence-based (documented when possible) and unemotional (neutral terminology, not based on feelings). There are two main reasons for this:

1. You don't yet know the reason for the under-performance, so you cannot legitimately express negative feelings.
2. Any expression of feelings that the person interprets as personal criticism will make them less likely to assist in resolving the problem.

You can legitimately express annoyance or disappointment, but make it clear that these feelings are directed at the results, not at the person.

As this process unfolds you may discover that the under-performance has happened due to factors outside the person's control.

There are three basic reasons that a person's performance will fail to meet your expectations:

1. **They don't know how to do it**. Perhaps one of you overestimated their capability when the task was allocated, or additional unforeseen difficulties have emerged. As a manager you need to become aware of these possibilities and take remedial supportive action.
2. **They don't want to do it**. This could be a general issue of their overall motivation towards their job, or it could be that they have conflicting priorities (particularly if they are managed by several people) and are unsure about the importance you attach to this specific achievement. Either way, you need to find out the reason and take some action.
3. **Something is stopping them doing it.** As a manager you do not know all the detail of how the work actually gets done. In all organisations there are procedures, protocols and personalities which are sometimes in conflict. This type of discussion can often be a useful way of gaining information about how things really work, and whether you need a managerial intervention to make improvements.

Here are some good examples of how to start the conversation:

"The target for customer contact calls is 50 per

week. For the last two weeks your average has been 30..."

"When we talked last week you agreed to send me the report by Wednesday. I received it on Friday..."

Note that the manager restricts the opening gambit to simple statement of fact, without expressing any judgemental emotion. The message this conveys is, "I accept that there could be a valid reason, but I need you to tell me what it is."

Here are some bad examples:

"I'm not happy with the volume of calls that you are making..."

"You don't seem able to meet deadlines..."

Note that although these openings still refer to objective facts, they are much less specific and there is direct or implied criticism of the person.

Here is a really bad, though sadly quite common example:

"You're not pulling your weight. Hit the target or hit the road."

2. Probe for causes. Note answers. Summarise for completeness and understanding

Once you have made it clear what the discussion is to be about, you can move to this step of finding out what reasons they want to give. They may not want to tell you the real reasons, or all of the reasons. Quite often in organisations there are problems which staff would prefer to sort out for themselves without involving their manager. If necessary, let this happen. For this management process to work, you don't necessarily need the full story. In fact, you don't even need a true story. This is not a police interrogation. Again, your tone should be neutral. A good opening statement is:

"So, I need to know the reason for this."

Asking for a reason feels less antagonistic than asking "Why...?" It says to the other person, "There may be a perfectly reasonable explanation, and I would like to know what it is so that I can help if necessary."

Your first question may yield all the information you need, but be prepared to ask follow up questions if necessary. The purpose of follow-up questions is twofold.

Firstly, it gives you extra detail which may be necessary for helping with the problem-solving.

Secondly, if they are telling a story which is not entirely true, it gets them used to the idea that it is actually easier to tell the truth. Your (unspoken) attitude at this stage should be, "If that's what you want to tell me, that's what I'm going to put on the record."

It is also very important at this stage that you refrain from challenging the reasons that they are giving you. This is particularly tempting if the reason that they give implies some criticism of your own managerial actions or style.

The other very important thing is to not offer a fix for the problem. Again this is very tempting, particularly if you know that the solution is very simple. The purpose of this interaction is to assist the person to solve their own problem. Telling them the solution or what to do undermines their belief in themselves as a capable human being. It also rewards them for bringing you problems to solve, so they will tend to do it more frequently up to the point where you are doing virtually all their job, and have no time left for your own.

Whatever reason they give for what they have done, write it down and carry on with subsidiary questions, or probing for any other reasons.

When it is clear that you have exhausted what they can tell you about the cause(s), summarise back to them what they have told you:

"So let me just check that I've got this clear... Is that right?" It is important to remember that any feelings they have expressed are also facts that need to be reflected back, to ensure that you have recorded them correctly.

Summarising their responses gives you control of the discussion, and enables you to move on to the next swift but very important step.

3. Ask the person for help to solve the problem

This apparently simple request achieves a wide range of positive effects. So it is important to remember to include it.

1. Asking for their help boosts their self-esteem, making them feel a valued contributor to the problem-solving process.
2. Describing it as a problem reinforces the fact that it **is** a problem. It will not go away, and it has to be solved.
3. Treating the discussion as a problem-solving exercise relieves the person of blame, and makes

them more likely to contribute positive suggestions.

4. It emphasises that the **performance** is the problem. The **person** is part of the solution.
5. It gives them ownership of both the problem and the solution, i.e. it tells them that the problem is theirs, not yours. Your role is to support them in solving their problem.
6. They are far more likely to succeed with a solution that they feel they have created, rather than one they have been given.

4. Ask for and note possible solutions. Evaluate suggestions

This is the stage where you can start identifying possible solutions to the problem.

However, it is important to keep the solutions and the discussion separate.

Keep on asking for suggestions until you have enough to work on, and then start discussing them.

Ask (note), ask (note), ask (note)... discuss, discuss, discuss.

The reasons for keeping suggestions and discussion separate are:

1. The first solution offered may not be the best one.
2. If you start discussing a proposed solution prematurely you are likely to get bogged down in detail.
3. If you discuss a proposed solution and find that it won't work, you have ended the discussion on a negative. The person is then less likely to generate other ideas.
4. Some proposed solutions may trap you into doing work that should not "belong" to you. Although you must become involved if the solution does require an action that only you can undertake, the main emphasis of this exercise is to support the person in identifying the actions that they need to take to resolve their own problems.

Simply note each suggestion as it occurs, using follow-up questions only to clarify, not to evaluate.

It is important to refrain from telling them your own ideas for a solution. Only ever do this if the person is totally unable to think of one of their own. Even then introduce it indirectly. Use phrases like:

"Have you ever considered doing...?"

"Others who've had this problem found it helpful to... Do you think that might help you?

This will get you to a point where you have something to discuss. Once they start discussing the action they start to own it.

Once you have a number of suggestions listed, you can then start to evaluate them. Whenever possible your evaluative questions should reflect ownership back to the other person, e.g.

"How do you see that working...?"

"Is there anything else you need to do before that...?"

The more active the person is on working out the technicalities of the solution, the more successful they are likely to be in practice.

Some suggestions may attempt to pass tasks in your direction. Be wary of this because you should not take on somebody else's job. On the other hand, be open to the fact that small changes in the way you operate could make a great difference to the effectiveness of others.

Once you have evaluated the proposed solutions (and maybe edited out one or two), you move out of collaborative problem-solving mode into managerial mode by identifying what it is that you want the person to do. Thank them for their ideas and move on to the next step.

5. Decide and note specific actions

At this point you are in a position to make a decision about what you want the person to do.

This may on the surface look like you are giving an order, and thus violating one of the principles of human behaviour; that people do not like being told what to do.

In fact, what you are doing is selecting the action(s) that they have already suggested and gaining their commitment.

It is important to distinguish between **agreement** that something would be a good idea, and actual **commitment** to perform an action.

A useful phrase is:

"So, what I'd like you to do is…" It is important to write down the specific action(s), timing and deadline because you will need these for subsequent meetings.

Follow that with confirmation of their commitment to perform the action(s) by using a phrase like:

"Will you do that?"

The answer needs to be "Yes," not "I'll try." "I'll try," means, "I want to keep failure as an acceptable option."

Gaining commitment is important because you will need it to manage the person through the Follow-Up set of steps at subsequent meetings.

You now have now:

Identified the problem,

Identified the cause(s),

Identified the solution,

Gained commitment to implementing the solution,

Set a timetable for action(s).

All that remains is to set a date and time for your next meeting. So move on to Step 6.

6. Set date and time for follow-up

The purpose of the next meeting will be either,

1. To give them some form of recognition that they have resolved the problem, and thus reinforce the performance improvement, or,
2. To present evidence of continued under-performance, and go through a similar but more forceful process (a Follow Up meeting) to tackle the performance issue.

So set the date and time in your diaries.

Thank the person for their help and express your confidence that they will resolve the problem.

"Thanks for your help. I'm sure that what you propose will sort out the problem. I'd like us to meet again on (date/time) for an update about how you're getting on."

Make sure that you keep your commitment about the follow-up session.

Between now and the follow up date you will need to gather further information about their performance following the meeting. You do not need to gather information about whether they have implemented their action commitments. They may not have told you the truth about the reason(s) for the original problem, so the proposed solution might just be a fiction. But if they have resolved the performance issue by whatever means, it doesn't really matter. Only if they have failed to improve performance do you need to look at the commitments again.

Consolidation:

Memorise the steps of the process:

1. Describe specifically the problem.
2. Probe for causes. Note answers. Summarise for completeness and understanding.
3. Ask the person for help to solve the problem.
4. Ask for and note possible solutions. Evaluate suggestions.
5. Decide and note specific actions.
6. Set date and time for follow-up.

Use the template to plan and rehearse how you would tackle a performance-management issue from your own current or past experience.

If you cannot think of any examples, use this one:

Manager:

You recently delegated the production of the monthly report to one of your staff. Although they were initially enthusiastic, you now find that the

reports are coming in later than they should. When you do get the report, you have to spend some time editing out a lot of unnecessary detail. You have mentioned this several times, but the problem seems to be getting worse.

Employee:

You were happy to be given the task of producing the report, because it acknowledged your managerial potential by giving you an overview of how the department operates. You are putting a lot of effort into this task. As a potential manager you feel it is important to demonstrate your understanding of the department. Sometimes this is difficult when collating information from areas that you are not entirely familiar with because you are not sure what is important or not, so you think it is better to include all the data you are given. Your manager has mentioned that the reports have been a bit long-winded, but you don't want to miss out anything important.

ADDITIONAL APPLICATIONS

Obviously the steps in this module are designed primarily for situations where you manage the performance of a member of your staff.

However, because the process is based on fact not feelings, it can also be applied effectively in situations where you have no direct authority.

Colleagues:

Often the success of your work depends on colleagues and co-workers performing their work to a particular standard, or meeting commitments that they have made to you. If they let you down, you can use these steps to improve their performance.

Your manager:

Sometimes you might find that your manager does things, or fails to do things, making it more difficult for you to do your job. If you have the courage, you can use these steps to manage your manager. It's not as difficult as it sounds because you share the same interest in getting results as effectively as possible.

Suppliers and Customers:

If you find that customers or suppliers are doing things that make it difficult to work with them, this process could help you both work out a solution, without jeopardising the relationship.

Family:

In general, it is not advisable to use managerial techniques on family members. However, there are occasions (particularly with teenagers) when this set of steps is a lot more effective than shouting at them.

These additional applications also work for Behaviour Management.

BEHAVIOUR MANAGEMENT

Steps of the process:

1. Describe specifically the behaviour problem.
2. Explain the reason it concerns you.
3. Probe for causes. Listen and respond with empathy.
4. Explain the need for change. Ask for and record ideas.
5. Discuss each idea. Express your support.
6. Decide and record action(s) and timing. Set a follow up date.

In other parts of this programme we use the term "behaviour" in a technical sense to refer to "things that people do or say", in the context of this technique its use is overlaid with a notion of unacceptability (bad behaviour).

Managing poor behaviour is more complicated than managing poor performance. It is relatively easy to decide whether to take managerial action concerning a person's performance, because there is usually an objective level of achievement which is either attained or not.

With poor behaviour, it is often more difficult to determine whether a specific piece of behaviour represents something that comes within your remit as a manager.

Obviously, there are some forms of behaviour such as dangerous working practices which are easy to identify, and which must be addressed, but quite often your recognition of other forms of behaviour as a potential managerial issue builds up slowly and it is difficult to decide whether, or when, to take action.

One instance of the behaviour might be a surprise. Two or three instances might be a bit irritating. Four or more might be a habit.

The basic rule to go by is:

1. If the behaviour is not causing you a business problem, just learn to live with it, or try to regulate it by informal means.
2. If you believe that the behaviour may continue, or escalate to cause a business problem, you ought to tackle it.

3. If it is **actually** causing you a business problem now, you've got to fix it.

How do you tell whether behaviour is a business problem, and not just something that irritates you?

Behaviour is a business problem when:

1. It is an infringement of company rules or against company policy.
2. It interferes with the ability of others to perform their work effectively.
3. You have received a complaint.
4. You have tried, and failed, to correct the problem behaviour by informal means.

In principle, a behaviour issue can be tackled just the same as a performance issue. The structure of the interaction is almost identical to that of performance-management.

The main differences are:

1. Sometimes people are unaware of their behaviour or its effect on others, so your raising the issue may be a surprise to them.

2. People often regard their behaviour as an integral part of their personality, and regard criticism of their behaviour as criticism of them as a person.
3. The reasons underlying the behaviour can be complex and sometimes raise sensitive issues. Therefore, you need to be more delicate in your approach. You need to plan the interaction thoroughly, and use all the interpersonal skills.

1. Describe specifically the behaviour problem

Be specific and use precise details. Refer to records or other documentation, reliable witnesses or your own observations.

Be careful to use phrases which are less likely to be perceived as personal criticism. Remember it is the behaviour, not the person that is the problem.

"Yesterday, and this morning, you arrived at the office after 9.15."

"Earlier this morning I saw you cross the factory floor without a safety helmet."

These examples are more specific and behavioural than:

"You seem to be getting a bit lax on your timekeeping."

"You are not adhering to the safety regulations."

There is no need to express any emotion in your description of the behaviour. The fact that this is your opening gambit in a recognisably managerial context is sufficient to convey the seriousness of the situation.

2. Explain the reason it concerns you

Some forms of behaviour are self-evidently a problem that you have a right to be concerned about. In other cases, the business reason for tackling it may not be obvious to the other person.

In nearly all cases, the person will have some sort of justification for their behaviour.

By explaining your reasons for tackling the problem **before** you start analysing the causes, you reinforce your position as the manager. You will later be asking them about their reasons for the behaviour. This step helps you to emphasise that, whatever those reasons may be, they are not going to be accepted as excuses. This is not the same as saying that they are **invalid reasons**. All reasons are "valid" in the sense that they are what the person says is the cause of their behaviour.

The reasons may be understandable. The behaviour

is not acceptable, and is causing you a problem.

3. Probe for causes. Listen and respond with empathy

Now that you have made it clear that the behaviour is causing a business problem you can look into what is causing the behaviour.

In many cases the behaviour causing the problem is simple to explain and to remedy. For example, the person may not even have been aware of what they have been doing, or that it was causing a problem.

In most other cases the causes can be quite complex and overlaid with emotional issues.

Assuming that the person is aware what counts as acceptable and unacceptable behaviour in the workplace, they will put forward a rationale which "justifies" the behaviour that you have identified as problematic.

In some cases, the person may express the view that some poor behaviour is allowable because of their excellence in other parts of their job. People with high levels of expertise in their main area sometimes show poor behaviour towards other people who are not at the same level of expertise, or those that they see as being in a support role.

In almost all other cases, poor behaviour will be found to be related to something stressful happening in the workplace or in their life outside work.

You are not allowed to ask questions about their domestic life, unless they offer the information first. Even then, be very careful. You are their manager, not their counsellor. Your only legitimate concern is how it affects their behaviour at work.

You will need to ask probing subsidiary questions in order to ascertain the facts as they appear from the other person's point of view.

Your probing questions need to take account of the fact that people may be reluctant to give you the full story, or even the real story. People often try to confuse the situation by giving related facts that they think they might be able to get away with e.g. "I know I was late; there were road works at the main junction."

For management purposes you only need a story. Your management of the behaviour can succeed even if it is based on a partial or a false story.

The purpose of the probing is to get near to the facts if you can. The subtext of the probing is, "Yes you can get away with telling me things that are either untrue or only partly true, but it is going to be hard work to make it hang together."

Those facts will usually have emotions attached to them, so use empathy to move the discussion along.

Make a note of the facts given, because you will need to refer back to their story if you have to tackle the issue again. In summarising what they have told you, make sure that you use empathetic behaviour (accurately labelling the emotion expressed) and move on.

4. Explain the need for change. Ask for and record ideas

No matter what the cause of the behaviour, the behaviour itself is unacceptable and needs to change, otherwise you would not be having this meeting.

Although the person's behaviour may be understandable, for the reasons given in the previous step, you cannot allow the behaviour to continue (for the reasons that you gave in the second step).

This step makes it clear that, whatever the reasons given, the person needs to change their own behaviour, and you need to draw out their suggestions for doing so. In cases where the behaviour is due to some interpersonal conflict, you may need to have a similar conversation with the other person involved. That will be a separate management task, and does not diminish the need for the current person to change their own behaviour.

Behaviour is in some ways a more sensitive issue than performance, so the ideas the person produces are likely to be more tentative, using phrases like: "Well, I suppose I could try..."

It is important to encourage the production of ideas by appropriate use of verbal cues. Silence is also a useful tool for encouraging the production of further ideas.

Simply write down the ideas, without analysis or comment. Just like in the process for performance-management, it is important to leave discussion of individual ideas until no other ideas are forthcoming.

Remember that the ideas don't have to be the things that **you** would do to control **your** behaviour. It is the other person who needs to take ownership of changing **their** behaviour, so they need to come up with some sort of self-control mechanism that would work for them.

Only if the person is unable to generate any potentially workable solution should you input any of your own.

As with performance-management, you should beware of "solutions" which put the onus back on you. For example, if person A cannot get along with person B, A might propose a solution involving you in rearranging work schedules so that they don't have to interact. This is not a solution. The solution is for A (and possibly B, as a result of a separate discussion) to change their behaviour so that collaboration is possible, at least during working hours.

You need to offer, rather than impose, ideas by using phrases like:

"Have you considered...?"

"How would you feel about...?"

"I was once in a similar situation, and what I did was..."

When you have completed this step, and have a suitable range of ideas, you can move on to the practicalities of implementing one or more of them.

5. Discuss each idea. Express your support

Up to this point, the discussion of solutions has been hypothetical. Now it is time to start making one or more of them a reality.

You need to lead the person into talking about

what they would actually need to do to make the solution happen, so you may need to ask them some questions on how they would go about it.

Discuss the other person's ideas. Use their workable ideas if possible. If their ideas are not workable, explain the reason that you cannot use them, and discuss your own as part of the general set of ideas.

Once they have committed to a particular alternative behaviour, make a note of that commitment because you may need to remind them of it in subsequent meetings.

The chances are that they will have come up with a solution that will work, and you can monitor subsequent behaviour to find out whether it has worked.

On the other hand, their whole story could have been a fiction and their "solution" just something they said to get out of the situation. This does not really matter. They have made a commitment to change their behaviour. So long as the behaviour becomes acceptable, how they do it is unimportant.

Expressing your support does not mean that you have taken ownership of their problem. All it means is that you will do what you can to help them resolve their work-behaviour problem. It simply reinforces the sentiment that you want them to succeed.

There may be parts of the solution that require your intervention, such as having a similar conversation with person B'. This can be quite useful because it conveys the message, "I will keep my commitment to you, and I expect you to keep yours to me."

6. Decide and record action(s) and timing. Set a follow up date

This is where **you** decide on the most appropriate action to resolve the problem, and gain the person's commitment to implement it. It is important to ensure that the person understands their accountabilities (and yours if appropriate), and that they make a definite commitment.

It may feel like you have already done this in the earlier stages, but it is important to boil the whole discussion down to one positive statement, e.g.

"You say that when X happens you could do Y, and not Z. Will you do that?"

As with performance-management, "I'll try," is not a positive commitment. "Yes," is the only acceptable answer.

As part of your final summing up it is important to set time parameters, and a date for your next meeting.

Before the next meeting, continue to obtain evidence of successful or unsuccessful behaviour-change.

Use the next meeting either to give positive reinforcement of their success/progress (Praise and Recognition), or to take the next step to resolve the problem (Follow-Up).

Consolidation:

Memorise the sequence of steps:

1. Describe specifically the behaviour problem.
2. Explain the reason it concerns you.
3. Probe for causes. Listen and respond with empathy.
4. Explain the need for change. Ask for and record ideas.
5. Discuss each idea. Express your support.
6. Decide and record action(s) and timing. Set a follow up date.

You may be lucky and have no current behavioural issues that you need to address. It is almost certain that you will at some point encounter unacceptable behaviour requiring managerial intervention.

Typical examples are:

1. Recurrent lateness or poor timekeeping.
2. Persistent failure to meet deadlines.
3. Excessive time spent on personal business.
4. Inappropriate use of company resources.
5. Behaviour which lowers the morale of colleagues.

Spend some time planning how you would tackle these, paying particular attention to specific behavioural commitments which could lead to elimination of the problem.

As an example of questioning leading to commitment, consider the following:

An employee has been late to work twice in the last week. When asked for the reason he explains that his wife has just returned to work and he is now responsible for taking their children to the childminder. The extra journey sometimes takes him longer than he thought it would due to unfamiliar traffic conditions.

This is acceptable as a reason, but not acceptable as an excuse. It may not be the whole story, or it may even be a complete lie.

Whatever doubts you may have about whether you have been given the real reason, it is not legitimate to probe for information about the person's domestic circumstances.

For managerial purposes all you need to do is note down the given reason. You then remind him that you do need him to be at work on time, and ask for his ideas to make sure that he does this.

Typical suggestions might include using a different route, setting off earlier etc. Whatever he suggests, you obtain his commitment to implement the solution and make a note of what it was.

At the very least this means that he is not able to use the childminder travel as a reason for any further lateness. He also knows that his timekeeping is under scrutiny, so even if the actual reason was related to some other problem which he has not disclosed, he had better take action to resolve it.

TAKING FOLLOW UP ACTION

Steps of the process:

1. **Describe the problem specifically.**
2. **Describe specifically the lack of improvement; probe for reasons and information.**
3. **Ask for, discuss, and record possible solutions.**
4. **Explain the consequences of no improvement.**
5. **Decide and record specific action and timing. Set follow up date.**
6. **Express confidence in the person to resolve the problem.**

When you have taken action to improve performance or behaviour, you have started a process which must continue until you have achieved a positive outcome. So you need to have further meetings. In some cases, the appropriate type of meeting will be a Progress Review, where they report back to you how they are getting on. In other cases, where you already have information that they have succeeded in resolving the problem, you will need a Praise and Recognition meeting to reinforce their achievement.

When you have information that leads you to believe they have not made progress on changing their performance or behaviour, you need to use the Follow-Up technique, described below.

This is where you reinforce the message that you are still "on their case", and that the management process is now becoming more serious in terms of the consequences.

The style of the Follow-Up meeting remains the same as the previous meeting(s) in that it is to be conducted in the same, unemotional, problem-solving manner, but it contains a more serious reminder that things have to change and that the process will continue until the situation is resolved.

The positive outcome of this interaction is either the person will now recognise the seriousness of the need for improvement, and will take action to change their performance/behaviour, or they will make no/insufficient improvement and move themselves one step closer to some form of disciplinary action.

You can also use this set of steps as a first discussion when an offence is serious enough to warrant disciplinary action for any further occurrence.

1. Describe the problem specifically

The problem is now bigger than it was originally. You have the original problem of the unsatisfactory performance/behaviour, but you now also have the fact that at the previous meeting they made a commitment to implement their ideas for correcting the situation.

The fact that you are now having this meeting means that something did not work, and for some, as yet unknown reason, they haven't made the correction.

There are a limited number of reasons the improvement has not happened:

1. They have taken no action, or insufficient action. This often happens when people are used to a manager "blowing hot and cold". They hope that you will become immersed in some other issue so that you will forget to focus on this problem. So now you have the additional issue of their failure to keep to their commitments.

2. They did take the action(s), but the result was not as anticipated. This is perfectly understandable.

Business life is full of problems. Solutions are attempted; some work, others do not. This simply means that more effort is needed to find another solution which will work.

3. The reasons given for the original problem were not the full story, so the remedies were irrelevant. This is why it is important to take notes of every meeting so that you know what questions you asked and what they actually said.

4. Something else. It is important to be emotionally neutral during this meeting. Although the problem may not be as simple as you originally believed, it is still just a problem; and the correct approach to a problem is to treat it as a problem-solving exercise.

So, simply refer back to the original meeting, and describe:

1. The original problem.
2. The reasons given.
3. The commitments made.

Then move on to the current situation.

2. Describe specifically the lack of improvement; probe for reasons and information

The current situation is that, despite your previous discussion, there has been a continuation of the performance/behaviour problem.

It is important that your description of the lack of improvement must be evidence-based, referring to specific information gained since the last meeting.

Of course you may be disappointed that the expected outcome has not been achieved, but if you express disappointment in the person, or criticism of them, they are unlikely to be positive about resolving the problem.

Your questions need to focus firstly on these issues:

1. Did they do what they said they were going to do? If not, what is the reason that they didn't.
2. How did they go about it? Were there parts of the solution that worked, and others that didn't.
3. If they fulfilled their commitments, what do they think is the reason it didn't work? Asking for a reason, as opposed to the more accusatory "Why?" has the effect of reassuring the person that you are on their side in helping them to find something

that will work (to resolve their performance/behaviour problem).

Your initial questions, and subsidiary probing, will give you a reasonable idea about whether the solution will involve:

1. Putting more effort into fulfilling the original commitments, or,
2. Finding some other commitments.

3. Ask for, discuss, and record possible solutions

It is important to bear in mind at this stage what the actual problem is.

One type of problem is that lack of satisfactory progress is due to the fact that the "solutions" you both agreed at the previous meeting were implemented but were not sufficient to resolve the issue. In this case, you need to re-visit the original problem and ask for further ideas for solving it.

Otherwise, you are not now interested in the original problem except as background to your current discussion.

The other type of problem that now needs a solution is how to get the person to fulfil their commitment to implement their original solution that was agreed at the last meeting, i.e. how can they make themselves do what they said they were going to do.

This emphasis gives the person the message that you are not going to let the problem go away.

Your manner should be supportive, not aggressive.

The person has had a problem implementing the commitments that they made. Your role is to help them resolve that problem.

Use verbal and non-verbal cues to encourage the flow of ideas.

Take notes on the ideas as they emerge, and only start to discuss or examine individual ideas once a sufficient number have been generated.

4. Explain the consequences of no improvement

If the person has not yet realised that you are serious about resolving the problem, this step will confirm it.

This is where you tell them **what you will do** if there is no improvement.

Depending on the circumstances there will be a range of actions that you can take, and you must by this stage be certain that you can **and will** implement the consequence.

The consequence needs to be an action.

If you are managing an employee, the consequence is likely to be that you will apply some form of sanction, or take the first step of a disciplinary procedure. In most disciplinary procedures the first step is a verbal warning. Some require a "warning of a warning". Some offer the option of a supportive witness. Check with your HR department or staff handbook if you are not certain.

If you are managing a supplier or a customer your sanctions would probably relate to revising the terms of your relationship.

Many managers feel they need to soften the blow of this step by making the consequence sound indefinite. This is counterproductive. It is important to make this step unambiguous. Whatever it is that you are going to do, say that you will do it.

There is a considerable perceived difference between:

1. "I may have to consider giving you a verbal warning," and,
2. "I will give you a verbal warning."

Although this step is assertive, it should be stated without emotional overtones. It is not to be perceived as a threat; just a statement of fact.

If you actually need to apply the sanction at a later stage, the person cannot then claim that they were not advised.

5. Decide and record specific action and timing. Set follow up date

From your notes of the discussion, identify the most workable idea(s) and recap what they mean in behavioural action terms.

You need to set a reasonable time-period for the person to activate their ideas, and you will need to monitor their behaviour/performance for any indication that they are having the desired effect.

Of course, you need to set an appointment for another meeting into your diaries. The format of the next meeting depends on the degree of change in performance/behaviour.

It could be a Progress Review if the change-period is long term. It could be a Praise and Recognition session to reinforce whatever progress or achievement they have made.

It could be a Disciplinary meeting to implement the sanction that you advised them about.

6. Express confidence in the person to resolve the problem

This meeting will not have been very comfortable for the other person. Even though you will not have expressed negative emotions, the structure and content of the meeting, together with the forewarning of a sanction, will have lowered the person's self-esteem.

If you want them to put effort into resolving the problem, it is important to boost their confidence in their ability to do so.

So it is necessary to include this step because you actually do want them to succeed, even if only for the reason that it makes more sense to "repair" existing staff than to find new ones.

So (find your own words), some words like, "I really want you to succeed at this, and I know you can do it if you set your mind to it," really do have an effect out of all proportion to their blandness.

If the person fails to resolve the problem, and you have to take disciplinary action, they cannot subsequently claim that you were not supportive. A large proportion of Constructive Dismissal cases hinge upon whether Management was supportive in helping the person resolve performance/behaviour issues.

Even if you are not fully confident, (maybe you doubt their capability or motivation) that the person will actually succeed with the commitments they have made, you need to say something positive to demonstrate your support. Sometimes, in order to act like a manager, it is necessary to **act** like a manager.

Consolidation:

Memorise the steps of the process:

1. **Describe the problem specifically.**
2. **Describe specifically the lack of improvement; probe for reasons and information.**
3. **Ask for, discuss, and record possible solutions.**
4. **Explain the consequences of no improvement.**
5. **Decide and record specific action and timing. Set follow up date.**
6. **Express confidence in the person to resolve the problem.**

An employee has had two behaviour management interviews concerning their late

arrival at work. In both interviews the reason given was that they had problems with their car, and they gave an undertaking that they would get the car serviced. Today they arrived late again. Use the template to prepare for a follow-up meeting.

As a manager, it is not your job to help them diagnose what is wrong with their car. Your only interest in the car is, "Did they do what they said they would do?" and "Did it make any difference?"

Remember that even if you find that they have not had the car serviced and have just done a bit of DIY tinkering, you are not entitled to instruct them to book a proper service.

If the reason given this time is something other than the unreliable car, would you consider starting the behaviour management process again? If not, why not?

TAKING DISCIPLINARY ACTION

Steps of the process:

1. **Describe the problem, review previous meetings and commitments.**
2. **Probe for reasons and information. Listen and respond with empathy.**
3. **Document the information and summarise.**
4. **Explain the action that you are taking, and the reasons.**
5. **Discuss and document future behaviour needed. Set follow up date.**
6. **Express your confidence that they can correct the behaviour.**

Please bear in mind that throughout this chapter, and the whole programme, disciplinary action is part of an improvement process, not a punishment. Although it is obviously not a pleasant experience for either the manager or the employee, there is no need to make it more unpleasant by expressing anger or belittling people.

Discipline as punishment is counterproductive for two main reasons.

Firstly, by deliberately making the person feel bad, you are likely to create a resentful response. People who feel resentful are not well disposed towards doing anything that their manager wants, such as improving their performance or behaviour. They also can become quite inventive in devising non-attributable ways of sabotaging their manager's achievements.

Secondly, it breeds an attitude of "Do the crime, serve the time", as if the receipt of a punishment somehow wipes the slate clean of their previous "offences".

Within Disciplinary Action, the application of a sanction is only a minor part of the process. The overall purpose of the process is to continue the attempt to assist a person in improving their performance or behaviour. The sanction is primarily there to serve as a reminder of the seriousness of the continuing situation. As a beneficial side-effect it also shows that you, as the manager, are prepared to fulfil the commitment that you made in the previous meeting. By implication, the other person ought to be able to fulfil the commitment that they made.

This set of steps is to be used:

1. When a previous follow up meeting has not produced the desired change in performance or behaviour, despite the person having made a commitment to do so.
2. If the person has committed an infringement of company rules which warrants immediate correction. Obviously, in this case you adjust the process to refer to the company rule rather than to previous meetings.

Many managers try to avoid disciplinary action because:

1. They fear the consequences of doing it wrong. Many unfair dismissal cases hinge upon how the disciplinary procedure was carried out rather than the issue about which the person was disciplined. You have to follow your own internal procedures, so check with your HR Department or Company Handbook to ensure you follow your own rules.
2. They prefer to delegate this task upward to their own manager, or to the HR Department. This is a

waste of effort because in the time it takes to brief someone else on the history and issues involved, the manager could easily have done it themselves. Some HR departments insist on conducting all stages of disciplinary action themselves. Partly this may be due to a desire to demonstrate their practical value to the organisation. Partly it may be due to their having had to clear up the mess caused by unskilled managers.

3. They are not yet sufficiently annoyed to take action. Most people are wary of entering what they feel will be an unpleasant encounter, and some will avoid doing so until they are properly "psyched up". This is an error, because anger and annoyance lead to mistakes in handling the process.

Although taking disciplinary action may be thought to be uncomfortable, both for the manager and the person on the receiving end, it need not be as hard as most managers anticipate.

It helps if you remember that disciplinary action is just one more stage on the way to resolving the performance or behaviour problem. Some people need to experience this stage before they feel a need to make a real effort, particularly if they have a history of working with managers who let the matter drop after a token display of improvement.

It is a positive step because the structure of this interaction is designed to produce a positive outcome one way or the other. Either the problem is resolved, or the disciplinary procedure continues towards dismissal.

Your mental stance on conducting this interview needs to be:

"At our last meeting you made a commitment to me that you would do X. I gave you my commitment that if you did not do X, I would do Y. You have not met your commitment, therefore I am meeting mine."

Any sanction you now impose was understood and agreed at the previous meeting.

1. Describe the problem, review previous meetings and commitments

Essentially, you provide the person with a summary of how the need for this meeting has come about. This consists of a brief history of the original problem, but more importantly a summary of the commitments that were made and which have not been kept.

Accurate notes of previous meetings are essential here, together with evidence of the continuation of the problem up to the last meeting, and further new evidence gathered since then.

It is important to use this summary to make it clear that this meeting is about one topic only, i.e. the continued failure to make a change in performance/behaviour. This is because of inadequate or non-existent application of their commitments.

In all people-management meetings, but particularly in anything involving discipline, it is important to stick to just one topic. As you gain more experience in this style of people-management, you will find that you have many simultaneous "threads" with the same person. For example, you could, in a meeting yesterday, have praised this same person for achievement in another aspect of their work. Keep the threads separate.

Once you have set the topic for the meeting, go to the next step.

2. Probe for reasons and information. Listen and respond with empathy

You are still primarily focussed on the process of helping the person to overcome their performance/behaviour difficulties.

Use questioning techniques to seek the reason that the unacceptable performance/behaviour is continuing.

Remember that your main focus at this stage is not the original problem. You have discussed this extensively in previous meetings.

Your main focus should be on the reasons that the solutions agreed in previous meetings have not resulted in an improvement.

However, be prepared to accept new information about the original problem. Quite often, people will not reveal the full story until they realise that their situation is becoming serious. If the person now wishes to give you a different story, accept it and use probing questions to ascertain the new facts.

It does not matter if the new story shows that the original story was untrue. You are a manager, not a police interrogator. Whatever the person wants to tell you is what goes onto the record.

It is possible that the person will express some sort of emotion in their explanation.

Do not challenge or discuss their emotion.

If you challenge their emotional statements, the interview will become an argument, and lose focus.

Simply recognise their emotion as a fact, by using empathetic behaviour, e.g. "You feel that I'm being hard on you," and move on.

3. Document the information and summarise

If new information has been disclosed which significantly affects your decision to impose a sanction, you have a couple of options.

You could abandon/postpone the disciplinary part, and proceed as if this were a new Performance/Behaviour-Management meeting.

Alternatively, you could impose a token sanction on the grounds that the unacceptable performance/behaviour has occurred, and then go back into helpful problem-solving mode.

If you have been given new information that requires further investigation, close the interview here and set a follow up date. The format of the next meeting will depend on what your investigation reveals.

Otherwise, this step is just to check that you have the account straight.

Read back the points from your notes, to check that you have recorded them accurately, that you understand what the person has said, and to show that the discussion stage is now over.

4. Explain the action that you are taking, and the reasons

At the previous meeting you told the person what you would do if the performance/behaviour was not improved.

This is where you do it.

The reason is simple; you said you would do it, and now you are doing it.

In some cases, it will be necessary to explain the implications of your action, depending on the severity of the sanction.

Most disciplinary procedures have a set of graduated steps, ranging from verbal warning to dismissal. Other sanctions might include removal of responsibilities or reduction of privileges.

It is important for the person to understand that this interview is just one in a continuing process.

The whole purpose of administering discipline is to focus the person's efforts on improving their performance/behaviour. It is not a one-off "punishment", and if necessary, you will use the next disciplinary step.

It is helpful if you remind the person of the next step and the overall structure of the disciplinary procedure.

Sometimes, in this type of interview, it is not always clear whether the sanction has actually been applied. This is particularly the case with verbal warnings.

Some managers might feel that the mere fact of having this meeting counts as a verbal warning.

Others might try to temper the blow by saying, "So, I'm going to give you a verbal warning." (Has the warning been given, or is this just a warning of a warning?)

Make it absolutely clear: "So I am now giving you a verbal warning that any further instances of... will result in..."

Do not go beyond this step until it the other person clearly understands that you have applied the sanction, and that they are aware of what the next sanction will be. When you are sure that they understand both the sanction and the process, make a note and proceed to the next step.

5. Discuss and document future behaviour needed. Set follow up date

By this stage you will have exhausted the analysis of the problem and so you can legitimately dictate your requirements because there is nothing further to discuss.

The person has had opportunities to give reasons for their poor performance/behaviour. They have given commitments to actions to remedy the problem. They have not remedied the problem. They have been given the promised sanction and told of further sanctions.

Now you just tell them what you want. This may be:

- a productivity target
- a behavioural target

or a detailed performance improvement plan. Although working under a performance improvement plan may carry a stigma, it is not a punishment; it is a management tool

Make sure you write down the details of what you have specified.

Use precise terms for the performance or behaviour required, not vague generalities like "improvement".

Make sure that the person understands.

Close the meeting by using the next step.

6. Express your confidence that they can correct the behaviour

This will be difficult if you have let your emotion drive your behaviour during this or previous meetings.

There is never any need to vent your emotion on the other person. By the time they get to this stage they will be feeling bad enough already.

It is important to let them know that, although they have been heading in the wrong direction, you still want to keep them within the team. As already mentioned, it is a lot cheaper to "repair" someone than to replace them. Also, they are probably not failing in all aspects of their job; just this particular thread. It is important to make them want to have acceptable performance/behaviour.

A manager's confidence is a great motivator. They know they have lost some of that by allowing matters to get this far, so it is important to say something positive which reminds them that they do have value.

An expression of confidence such as:

"I'm sure you'll be able to turn the situation round," will send them away feeling that they can return to the fold if they work at it. You may not entirely believe what you are saying, but say it anyway. It does no harm; it can help.

Close the meeting and continue monitoring. You may want to set a time limit on your monitoring. The danger with this is that after a period of acceptable performance/behaviour, the person might start to think of it as a "spent crime", and do it again.

It is up to you how hard a line you take on this. For example, if the unacceptable behaviour was to do with timekeeping it would be unfair to dismiss a person for being late for work again if there was a transport strike and everybody else was late that day.

You are allowed to exercise your judgement. That is why you are a manager.

If performance/behaviour returns to acceptable, use the next scheduled meeting to administer some praise, because you should be genuinely delighted that the process has worked.

Otherwise, proceed to next stage disciplinary action or dismissal.

Consolidation:

Memorise the steps of the process:

1. Describe the problem, review previous meetings and commitments.
2. Probe for reasons and information. Listen and respond with empathy.
3. Document the information and summarise.
4. Explain the action that you are taking, and the reasons.
5. Discuss and document future behaviour needed. Set follow up date.
6. Express your confidence that they can correct the behaviour.

Check your own organisation's disciplinary procedure with your Human Resources people, or the Staff Handbook, so that you are familiar with the details.

Hopefully, the need to impose disciplinary sanctions is quite rare. However, it would be useful to imagine situations where you might have to do so. A possible scenario you could work on is:

A = Manager, B = Employee

A. One of the company's safety rules states that anybody on the factory floor must wear a safety helmet. In the past this has often been ignored by office staff taking a short cut through the factory, but following a recent accident all the safety rules are being rigidly enforced. Some staff believe that this is unnecessary because they do not need to walk past any dangerous equipment, but most have complied.

One person in particular has been counselled twice (Behaviour Management), his only reason being that "he forgot". He said he would make every effort to remember. Last week you had a further meeting (Follow up) after another incident when he was seen not wearing a helmet, and you told him that if there were any further instances he would receive a verbal warning.

Yesterday you saw him bare-headed on the factory floor and asked him to come to your office this morning.

B. "People have been walking through the factory without helmets for years. It's a handy short-cut to the canteen when it's raining. This latest crackdown is stupid. The accident that triggered it was nothing to do with hard hats anyway. The regulation means that you have to sit with a hat all through lunch and then remember to bring it back afterwards. My manager just wants to be seen following the company line. This fuss will blow over in a few months as these things always do."

Consider also how long a period you might allow the warning of dismissal to continue. Obviously if the person was warned about dismissal last week and was caught again this week you would follow through with your promise. Would you feel the same after a month of compliance? Six months? A year?

DISMISSAL

Steps of the process:

1. **Describe the problem, previous meetings and commitments.**
2. **Probe for reasons for the continuing problem. Listen and respond with empathy.**
3. **Document relevant information and summarise.**
4. **Explain the disciplinary action and the reasons.**
5. **Stay calm and respond with empathy.**
6. **Specify how and when the dismissal will occur.**

Dismissal is the process that terminates your working relationship with a person. While it is primarily designed for terminating an employment contract, the same overall structure can be used for terminating any other contractual relationship.

It is a management **process**; not a single action. The "You're fired" model popularised in "The Apprentice" may be good entertainment but it is poor management.

This process is to be used when:

1. A series of meetings with the person, including all the appropriate steps of the disciplinary procedure, has not produced an acceptable change in their performance or behaviour.
2. The person has committed an offence sufficiently serious to warrant instant dismissal.

Of course, nobody is going to feel positive about using this process, but it need not be traumatic if it is conducted in a structured way.

It is important to follow the structure so that:

1. The other person is in no doubt about what is happening.
2. There is no possibility of doing something wrong, and invalidating the dismissal.
3. The likelihood of an emotional outburst is reduced.

1. Describe the problem, previous meetings and commitments

If dismissing someone for a serious offence, simply state the details of the offence, and skip step 2.

In all other cases, follow the procedure described.

It is vital that the person is made aware at the start what this meeting is about, and where it is going.

The review of the history of their commitments, your commitments, and the build up of the disciplinary process, lets them know how they have brought themselves to this stage. In a sense, it is not you who is dismissing them. The person has demonstrated that they are unable or unwilling to fulfil an essential part of their accountabilities, and effectively they are dismissing themselves.

It is important to stress the history of failure to meet commitments because the final reason for dismissing the person, taken out of context, may appear quite trivial.

The point is, however, that they are not here just because of one instance of unacceptable performance/behaviour. They are here for **one further** instance, after significant effort has gone into the attempt to remedy the problem.

Even at this late stage you should leave open the possibility that there could be some acceptable reason, so instead of going straight to dismissal, use the next step.

2. Probe for reasons for the continuing problem. Listen and respond with empathy

Here you are giving the person a last chance to come up with reasons that you have not heard before. Accurate notes from previous meetings are essential.

Sometimes people will take up this last opportunity to "come clean" because they now realise that the situation is really serious. For example, I know of one employee in a large company who was about to be fired for poor timekeeping, in particular taking extended lunch breaks, who "confessed" at this stage that he had been undergoing radiotherapy treatment. He had not wanted his colleagues to know, so had booked sessions for his lunch break instead of taking time off.

In most cases, however, the person will have nothing further to add. They may repeat some of the reasons that they gave at an earlier meeting, with added emotion or description of how difficult it has been to do what they said they would do.

It is important to keep this step free from discussion. All the appropriate discussions have been had at earlier meetings

Do not challenge anything that they say; just note it down and use empathy to move forward through any emotions they express.

If they provide new information which causes you to doubt that dismissal is appropriate, summarise and check that you have the details correctly, close the meeting and set a specific follow up date. This is not a cancellation. It is simply a postponement of the dismissal pending further investigation. The problem has not gone away, so your next meeting will need to be a Follow-Up, a Disciplinary Action, or a resumption of the Dismissal from the next step.

Otherwise proceed to the next step.

3. Document relevant information and summarise

The purpose of this step is twofold:

1. To provide the final record of the reasons for dismissal.

2. To make it clear to the person that their own behaviour has brought them to this stage.

You should have most of the information documented already, but you should add in any further observations made in step 2.

There is no need to summarise the whole history, as you have reviewed this at step 1. Just summarise the key points, ending with the commitment which you made at the previous meeting, i.e. the statement that continued poor performance or behaviour would lead to dismissal.

4. Explain the disciplinary action and the reasons

Essentially, your message to the person is:

"I said to you at our last meeting that if the performance/behaviour issue were to continue, I would dismiss you from the organisation. You have not resolved the problem, so I am now dismissing you." If using this process on non-employees such as suppliers, contractors (or even awkward customers) the final sanction would be termination of the contract; but the same principles apply.

Do not try to soften the blow by using imprecise words. It is essential for you to state clearly that the person is now dismissed.

With this statement you are emphasising that they are being dismissed not for this final instance of poor performance/behaviour, but for a continued history of failure to address the problem. In effect, they have dismissed themselves, but it is not helpful to state this.

You now have to cope with their reaction.

5. Stay calm and respond with empathy

In some cases, the build up of the disciplinary process has confirmed to the person that they are not able to do the job, or that they cannot conform to the required behaviour. Usually these people respond calmly. It is as if they just needed someone to give them the extra push rather than take the initiative by resigning. If so, go straight to the next step.

For many, however, the final realisation that they are dismissed does create a shock, and they are going to react emotionally.

Your empathy skills are essential at this stage. In most parts of this programme, empathy is used as a means of moving the discussion forward onto positive problem-solving. Here it is used as a means of putting them into an emotional condition where they can cope with factual information about the dismissal.

Surprisingly, unless you have said something crass, insensitive or critical, the person is highly unlikely to become aggressive.

Reactions will vary widely, so it is important to be able to identify the right emotional label for your empathetic responses.

Typical reactions may include:
1. Disbelief that the process has gone this far.
2. Anger (usually directed against themselves, but sometimes against the organisation).
3. Allegations of unfairness.
4. Asking for one last chance.
5. Concern about their forthcoming unemployment.
6. Concern about how to tell their partner/ family.

Just keep the tissues handy, and keep supplying the empathy until they are ready for the last step.

6. Specify how and when the dismissal will occur

Although you have already told them that they are dismissed, there are many factors affecting the "mechanics" how the dismissal occurs including:

1. Security of company information.
2. Risk of revenge (sabotage or theft).
3. Return of company property.
4. Notice period.
5. Final pay and benefits.

When you plan for this meeting, you need to check with you HR department or the Handbook, what your precise accountabilities are, and make a checklist to ensure that you do not forget any. This may be the last occasion you see this person, and it would be very awkward to have to contact them later to give them information that you forgot to mention.

You cannot rely on the person to prompt you with questions because they will still be in shock.

Working through a list of things that they need to be told, helps them come to terms with their new status outside the organisation. You also have a new status in that you are no longer managing this person. If appropriate you can leave your managerial mode aside and talk human to human, but remember not to say anything that could be interpreted (in a tribunal) as undermining the organisation or the dismissal process.

While nobody likes being fired, or firing others, conducting the process in this way will enable you both to get through it with the minimum of pain.

Consolidation:

Memorise the steps of the process:

1. **Describe the problem, previous meetings and commitments.**
2. **Probe for reasons for the continuing problem. Listen and respond with empathy.**
3. **Document relevant information and summarise.**
4. **Explain the disciplinary action and the reasons.**
5. **Stay calm and respond with empathy.**
6. **Specify how and when the dismissal will occur.**

Study your organisation's disciplinary procedure. It may be that you are not permitted to deliver the final dismissal. Some organisations

devolve this responsibility to the Human Resources experts. This is understandable because any procedural mishaps can invalidate the dismissal. Nevertheless, it is important to understand the procedure so that you can provide an accurate briefing for somebody else to perform the process.

Consider the case of the individual given a verbal warning for not wearing a safety helmet. The sequence of meetings, Behaviour Management, Follow Up, and Disciplinary Action, have got them to the point where they have been told that further instances will result in their dismissal. By this time the key issue is not the helmet. You are not taking the action because the person failed to comply with the safety regulation. You are firing them because they have persistently failed to meet the commitments that they gave you to change their behaviour.

www.ingramcontent.com/pod-product-compliance
Lightning Source LLC
Chambersburg PA
CBHW071420180526
45170CB00001B/169